There are dozens of books to guide the prospective buyer through the French legalities of house purchase. But once you have your home, what next?

Can We Afford the Bidet? is a guide to builders and buildings, bureaucracy and services, refurbishment and furnishing, and basic annual expenditure. It offers a few short cuts and several cautionary tales.

For the majority, a holiday home in France is a special kind of luxury, with sacrifices to be made; but sacrifices should only be relative to the fun of it all. It is easy to be carried away with temptations to embellish beyond immediate necessity – and purse. Elizabeth Morgan advises you never to lose sight of reality, to keep your head, and pace yourself.

A knowledge of French is useful, but a sympathetic attitude, a sense of humour plus a genuine desire to be friendly will compensate for any linguistic failures. Good neighbours are of paramount importance to the absentee householder.

The French are a delightful people, proud of their great heritage, and why shouldn't they be? They have much to be proud of. Often they are private and reserved, until you know them. Once you do, you have friends for life.

Elizabeth Morgan is not a lawyer, nor is she a property speculator, but over the past 20 years she has always had a holiday home in France. She has bought and sold three times, and in each house has had an unending experience of builders, plumbers, electricians, sharks and Honest Joes. She has made innumerable mistakes and miscalculations through inexperience, but friends, both French and English have proved invaluable tutors.

In *Can We Afford the Bidet?* Elizabeth Morgan passes on to others the distillation of her own experience and much of the advice that she has found so useful, blended with that essential ingredient – a sense of humour.

Throughout her professional life Elizabeth Morgan has worked in the entertainment business, as an actor/writer. Numerous television roles, include Sophie in 'The Old Devils', Joanna in 'We are Seven', Joyce in 'The Two of Us', Gina in 'Headhunters', several Dick Emery shows and many more. Theatre work includes her two one-woman plays, with which she has toured the USA, and stage roles at many UK venues including the National Theatre and Edinburgh Festival. Sha has also appeared frequently on BBC Radio and Television.

Elizabeth has worked extensively in BBC radio drama, and was in the EMI recording of 'Under Milk Wood' with Sir Antony Hopkins. She has written 26 plays for radio, including one for Vincent Price, plus several short stories. Her latest television play was 'Sisters Three', in which she also played a leading role.

She presented a children's TV programme for 18 months and provided the voices of Destiny and Rhapsody angel in the puppet series 'Captain Scarlet'. She is a regular voice-over artist for radio and television commercials and frequently dubs foreign films, preferring the French ones. She continues to write for magazines and newspapers. Currently she is working on a novel.

When she is not at her *chez nous*, she divides her time between London and her home in Chepstow.

Can We Afford the Bidet?

A guide
to setting up house
in France

Elizabeth Morgan

with illustrations by
Karin Littlewood

Lennard Publishing

First published in 1993 by Lennard Publishing
a division of Lennard Associates Limited
Mackerye End
Harpenden
Hertfordshire AL5 5DR

Paperback edition published in 1995

ISBN 1 85291 127 1

British Library Cataloguing in Publication Data
is available

Cover illustration by Karin Littlewood
Cover design by Paul Cooper
Editor: Caroline North

Printed and bound in Great Britain by
Butler & Tanner Ltd, Fome and London

Contents

Preface
to the Paperback Edition

Whenever a second edition replaces a first, inevitably with a book like this, certain changes and additions are to be expected in order to bring information up to date. As France has not had galloping inflation during the last two years, and the UK has not had an attack of prosperity, prices and equivalents indicated in the text, have remained roughly the same.

Banks

If you are suddenly short of francs and your French bank account is approaching the red, resist the temptation to call up your friendly UK bank manager for an urgent transfusion of liquid assets. This will cost you high bank transfer charges on both sides. Instead use your UK cash card in any French bank cash machine, provided both card and machine display similar symbols. Directions for use will appear on the screen in the language of your punched-in choice, and you will receive francs for the sum you have debited in sterling.

A word of warning about cash cards issued by your French bank, some cards will only operate in the department where your bank is located, so if your bank is in the Dordogne, you may not be able to draw cash from a machine in Calais. Remember to ask for a card carrying the universal cash icons.

France Telecom

If you should telephone a business organisation and their number is engaged, you could still be charged a nominal sum for the non-connection. This is not your fault, it is to do with the arrangement between certain companies and France Telecom. On one occasion, I tried, over the course of an hour, to make contact with Les Trois Suisse, a mail order company, finally with success. My detailed Telecom bill indicated that each of the half dozen or so abortive calls had been charged – not much, but enough to arouse caution in the future.

Getting there

If only we French house owners had houses in Spain instead, we could take cheap bucket-shop flights to Barcelona and Malaga, or even join organisations like Home Owners Abroad. But while ferry companies turn a blind eye to our ability to supply an increasing amount of bread-and-butter business for them *hors saison* and air companies make only negligible concessions, help is at last filtering through to us.

Competition between cross-channel ferries is keen, and becoming keener with Le Shuttle, and all to our advantage. Real bargains can now be found, particularly through companies like Eurodrive in North London (tel: 0181 342 8979), which act rather like brokers to the ferry companies. Whilst being able to guarantee discounts at any time of year, Eurodrive has a special relationship with Sally Line, being first to advise their clients of Sally's bargain offers (through this company in July/August '94, we crossed with car and passengers on Sally for £84 return). This year, '95, Eurodrive will not only be offering more bargain hovercraft flights and ferry crossings, but it is the only company at the present time holding promotions for Eurostar, the channel passenger train, and Le Shuttle, the car train.

Time was when nothing on earth would have persuaded me that crossing to my favourite country underwater could be better in any aspect than actually bouncing on it, give or take a touch of *mal de mer*. But I was wrong. The tunnel is smooth and fast, with immediate access to motorways on both sides. At both terminals there is a duty-free shop, albeit carrying less stock than the ferry and with limited services. But these are teething problems.

The evening we returned on the Shuttle, all channel surface crossings had been abandoned because of hurricane force winds and emptying heavens. Now we need no longer worry about the weather, we can nip across for a taste of *La Belle France* in mid-winter, or indeed at any time, with never a thought of cancellation or *mal de mer*. Progress indeed!

Elizabeth Morgan
Chepstow, February 1995

Introduction

There are dozens of books to guide us Brits through the French legalities of house purchase. But once you have your home, what next? You have realised the dream, certainly, but turning it into a practical reality, and not a nightmare, is another matter. It is not easy to sell a half-finished house, as some of my friends know to their cost. Many of the pitfalls they encountered could have been avoided if they had been forewarned.

This book is therefore designed to give new buyers, and potential buyers, a guide to builders and building, bureaucracy and services, refurbishment and furnishing, basic annual expenditure; and to offer a few short cuts, and several cautionary tales from which I learned the hard way.

Of course, if money is no problem, read no further, simply continue your good relationship with your chequebook. But for the majority, a holiday home in France is a special kind of luxury, with sacrifices to be made en route for the stake in the sun. But sacrifices should only be relative to the fun of it all. So take your time, and enjoy, enjoy!

There is something a little unreal about owning a holiday home, like playing house with Monopoly money. It's so easy to be carried away. Be it ever so humble, temptations to embellish beyond immediate necessity – and purse – are legion. So never lose sight of reality. Keep your head, and pace yourself. Remind yourself that this is a holiday home for two or three visits a year. If ever it should become your semi-permanent, or permanent retirement home, then presumably you would have a little more to spend. Without young children economy is not always such a pressing need, as many of us know.

I am not a lawyer, neither am I a property speculator, but over the past 20 years I have had a holiday home in France. We bought out first *ruine* – for *ruine* read hovel – for £900. It had no water, and no electricity. Since then I have bought and sold three times, and in each house I have had unending experience of builders, plumbers, electricians, sharks and Honest Joes. I have made innumerable mistakes and miscalculations through inexperience. Friends, both French and English, have proved invaluable tutors.

Throughout the vicissitudes of past years, with their share of joys and sorrows, the house in France has remained a constant. For my children it is an intrinsic part of their childhood, and now young womanhood. Despite the hours of elbow grease, sheer slog and months of planning, to say nothing of the inevitable doubts which crept in from time to time, my daughters and I feel so bound to our place in the sun that whatever unkind fate may befall, our house in France is the very last possession we should wish to lose. What started as a holiday home is gradually becoming more of a permanent home, at least in my affections. As time goes on, and the need to remain in Britain becomes less, the mere thought of escape to that glorious country, and for longer periods, is daily sustenance.

A knowledge of French is useful, but a sympathetic attitude, a sense of humour plus a genuine desire to be friendly will compensate for any linguistic failures. Good neighbours are of paramount importance to the absentee householder.

The French are a delightful people, proud of their great heritage, and why shouldn't they be? They have much to be proud of. Often they are private and reserved, until you know them. Once you do, you have friends for life.

Chapter One

The Basics

There has to be a starting point and houses, being as varied as their owners, will not all require basic living installations. However, the following guidelines are intended to accommodate those who may be starting with a *ruine*, as I did, rather than those two or more notches up the scale of house perfection.

Before your *chez vous* carries you away with what you would like to do/install/embellish/demolish, make a short list – as short as possible – of the absolute basics required. Then decide upon the sum you can afford, add on another third, and work forward or backward from there, eliminating or adding as you go. Always remember that the things you would like to do will come later. For the moment all you need is a habitable holiday base.

If the house has been empty for some time, you can be sure that water, electricity and gas will have been cut off. Country dwellers, obliged to use bottled gas, are at least able to cook immediately. The percentage of people in France using bottled gas is relatively high. Consequently there is a wide selection of *cuisinières* (cookers) designed with integral bottle housing. I know of a couple who brought their own gas cooker from the UK. It went back with them.

Gas and Electricity

You will find bottled gas in supermarkets and most garages. As in the UK, the first one is relatively expensive (about 291F); thereafter they are cheaper than in the UK, selling at between 60 and 70F a bottle. Even when I moved to a town, I did not forsake my country *cuisinière* for town gas. Bottles are remarkably economical, and seem to last forever, but always have a spare to hand, just in case your cousins arrive for a free holiday. And they do!

Having electricity (town and country), and gas (town) reconnected is very straightforward, as both are controlled by one organisation, located in the EDF (Electricité de France)/GDF (Gaz de France) office in your nearest town. You simply sign a contract, and arrangements are made, usually within 24 hours. You may be able to arrange the reconnection in advance, with the help of a reliable neighbour, friend or builder. Stumbling in the dark, especially with small children, is no fun, even if you know where the candles are kept.

Two years ago I arranged for my erstwhile builder to meet the EDF man at the new house, well in advance of my arrival. According to the builder, the EDF missed three appointments. According to the EDF, the builder was never there. I'm inclined to believe the latter, for when I arrived with friends, at nine o'clock one dark night, to find an even darker house, I went in hot pursuit of the builder. I found him, very drunk, in a local bar. He managed to drag himself to his feet, look suitably surprised at my presence, and suggest that my friends and I go to an hotel. In reply I suggested where he might go – permanently! It has been my good fortune never to have set eyes on that builder again.

Electricity in France is cheaper than in the UK. According to my bills – normal domestic tariff – the price per kilowatt has only increased from 0.46F in 1985 to 0.56F in 1992. The comparable figure in the UK in 1992 was 8.6p. Older houses frequently have no means of water heating and electrically heated water is therefore fairly commonplace, particularly where there is no piped gas. There are various systems; two common examples are an off-peak night tariff, operating between 10.30 p.m. and 7.00 a.m. at 32 centimes per kw, and a system whereby water starts to heat as the electricity supply is switched on at the mains. The water tank remains heated, and is simply kept topped up for the duration of the holiday.

According to the EDF, the former is better if you stay for a minimum of six months, the latter *plus intéressant* for a holiday home-owner. A useful phrase, *plus intéressant* (literally 'more interesting'), in this context means 'cheaper'. EDF bills are paid half-yearly.

Water

Eau et Assainissement (water and cleansing) is on a meter. When water is disconnected, the meter is taken and a new one supplied on reconnection. Two years ago when I moved into my village, the reconnection charges amounted to approximately £149. In the country it is not always easy to find the water bureau. Ours is a one-room brick building at the edge of a field, which took hours to locate. In town water charges are paid through the Bureau de Perception, usually an office in the Mairie.

When I was about to move from town into the country, like a good *citoyen* I went to the Bureau de Perception to give the name of the new owner for the registers and to give my forwarding address. Within moments a jubilant madame strode up and told me

I had 4500F to pay in retrospective water charges. I thought she was joking, and laughed, but unfortunately she was quite serious.

I have always paid bills almost as soon as they have arrived, and insisted that there had to be some mistake. She was adamant to the contrary, and by this time the whole office had shuffled around her in support. The charges covered 18 months, during which period I had made only two short visits to the house, alone. I suggested that it would have been cheaper to have bathed in asses' milk and laughed again. They did not. Clearly this was no laughing matter. I was told I would have to write out a cheque for the amount in question, or else the new owner of my house would have no water. This was particularly serious as my account was flat broke, I was due to return to the UK the next day and it would take several days to transfer money.

At this point I could see the shadow of the guillotine, so with shaking hands I wrote out a post-dated promise. There was no time to lose. I leaped up the stairs to the Water Office, where I met exactly the same routine. Another jubilant young woman with a computer came up with the same information.

I was apoplectic, particularly as all the counterfoils, my only means of defence, were in the UK. I took the name of the head of the department and promised to call him as soon as I got home. The young woman shrugged, and gave a smile of total disbelief, convinced she would never hear from me again. I was still smouldering as I crossed the Channel. But justice came to the rescue. Not only did I have all my water bills, all fully paid up, but I was able to double-check them against my old chequebook stubs.

I telephoned the office. There was some coughing, and an embarrassed silence. The chief was apparently not available, but the young woman informed me, very casually I might add, that they had confused me with another British family of the same name, and it was all sorted out, and of course I had nothing to pay, my cheque would be torn up. Was there an apology for the problems caused? Absolutely none, which proves that bureaucracy is the same insensitive animal everywhere. The lesson to be learned here is never, never throw away bill counterfoils for the main services, and always keep old chequebooks for at least three years.

The winter of 1986 was a particularly bad one, in which thousands of flamingos perished around the frozen *étangs* of the Carmargue. Our town too suffered in this exceptional freeze-up. I arrived in March to find that there was no water in the house. The meter, inside the door, had frozen up and cracked. There was no problem getting a replacement – the Mairie jumped to it immediately – but it is the householder who pays for it.

You may have to wait 24 hours for reconnection, depending on the time of year. This is where neighbours are invaluable. A few buckets go a long way. If the weather is warm, take the children swimming – they prefer it anyway – or use the showers in the nearest swimming pool. There was no hot water at my present house when we first arrived one very chilly April. But a plastic bucket filled from the kettle, used in the bathtub, is an effective substitute for a shower.

Water charges in France vary from region to region, with a surprisingly wide difference in price. For example, in the Paris region water is 10F a cubic metre, in the Normandy area it is 3F a cubic metre, and in the south-east 8F, which I am told is the national average. French water is all privately owned by a number of syndicates throughout the country.

I remember the first holiday in our primitive little *ruine*. It had been a swelteringly hot journey in high summer. The car was loaded with luggage, hot sticky children, and pools of liquid butter and chocolate, mixed together. Never was a family more in need of water in shower and kitchen. But, to our horror, there was none. And there was no one we could telephone because it was a Saturday afternoon. What is more, we couldn't even find the stopcock.

One by one our neighbours appeared to welcome us back, and through them we discovered the reason for our waterless house. There had been a problem during the winter and the *pompiers* (firemen) had turned our water off as a precaution. Never mind, we could turn it on again. Oh no, the stopcock was in the street under a manhole cover. But could we still turn it on? Oh no, it needed a special key which was at the Mairie. Exasperated, we then drove to the Commune's Mairie and fortunately the mayor was at home. Our key was not there but in the personal possession of the Chief Pompier. And where was he this blazing Saturday afternoon? At his nephew's wedding. Frantic phone calls ensued. One hour later a small wedding party turned up outside the house in an old Citroën. A smiling and, I thought, rather unsteady Chief Pompier disembarked holding aloft a giant sardine-tin key. Dressed in his wedding best, he nevertheless knelt on the dusty road with ne'er a thought for his knees, plunged his white-cuffed arm with key attached into the subterranean vault controlling our water, and turned the key. It took ten seconds. The children cheered, he beamed, the wedding party clapped and we felt like a lie down. We had water! But that was eighteen years ago, and nothing as dramatic, nor as colourful, has happened since – not with water, anyway.

The uses of the *pompiers* are multifarious. Their services to the community do not end with water taps. Soon after moving into my present house, I realised I was sharing it with wasps, which appeared to be nesting in the *grenier*'s beams. I did nothing, hoping they would leave me alone, as they were quite a distance from the living areas. In a day or two the builder arrived to cast an eye over immediate building requirements. He set foot in my kitchen at the same time that a little winged humbug, followed by a squadron of his mates, left his lofty nest on a daytime sortie. I was about to explain, in a lighthearted way, the whereabouts of my nesting visitors, but too late. Within those few seconds the builder had disappeared, vanished like the proverbial rodent from a ship in distress. I thought this a little lame for a big bearded fellow, but when I found him again, outside the house, he explained. It had been a long, hot, dry summer, and wasp stings were even more venomous without the dilution of water. There were rumours that a small baby had died from a sting. If I wanted him back I must first telephone the *pompiers*. By a stroke of luck the *pompiers* happened to be in the village at that very moment dealing with Mme Bonnet's *frelons* (hornets) - even more serious than my wasps.

When we located the *pompiers*, they were dressed, three of them, like spacemen. Their suits were heavily padded, trousers pushed into knee-high moonwalk boots. Their round helmets, with visors, appeared suitable for either bathysphere or spacecraft. From Michelin Man arms, huge gauntlets with courgette-size digits dangled. They each carried a fat syringe, about 18 inches long. The total effect was intimidating.

As soon as the hornets had been dealt a blow, they promised to visit my wasps, and the builder promised to return to the house. The *pompiers* behaved with impeccable military precision, and preparations for the attack were made quickly and quietly. The enemy had to be taken by surprise, they said. In silence, one of them holding a full syringe aloft, climbed the ladder to the *grenier*.

The others, poised below, syringes at the ready, were waiting for a rearguard action. We waited and watched while a solitary unsuspecting wasp returning home for a quiet evening led them to the nest. The *pompier* on the ladder whispered; 'Go in the kitchen, Madame, please. This could be dangerous.' The builder obeyed in an instant.

With a shout to his colleagues, Pompier One blasted his syringe into the beams. He descended the ladder quickly to allow Pompier Two to ascend and give another blast, followed by Pompier Three. I had been watching the action through the glass in the kitchen door, and as I came out, Pompier One yelled: 'Stand clear, Madame! Stand clear!'

With that a very large piece of honeycomb nest, full of dead wasps and eggs, crashed to the stone floor, followed by several more pieces. The *pompiers* inspected the result, and experience told them the nest was cleared. Satisfied, they removed helmets and gloves, shook hands, and promised there would be no recurrence. That was three years ago, and not a wasp has been seen visiting the old homestead since. This is a free service, I should add, paid for out of the local taxes.

Telephone

It took me 15 years to be finally seduced by France Telecom, and then it was solely on account of my elderly mum. Every time I head towards the Channel she develops withdrawal symptoms. An occasional chat on the telephone assures her that I am still earth side of the moon. The problem with a telephone in France is not you – because you have to pay for it – but the others, namely, offspring from adolescence onward. I have taken to hiding the telephone in the cellar's tool cupboard if one of the family happens to be arriving as I leave. This is not being mean, merely prudent, based on experience at home. A 15-minute chat, via French Telecom, about that dishy waiter, or swimming and sunbathing, to a best friend in London, is simply not on.

Telephone installation is rapid, and cheaper than in the UK. As far as my experience goes, there is no hanging about while Telecom check your financial credibility, and no one asks if you have been a subscriber before. The cost of installing a new line in a village or town is about £42. If your house stands alone in the middle of a forest, it could be more. Monthly rental is about £5.50. Local calls in France are reasonable, but of course the trouble with us foreigners is that most of our calls are likely to be expensive.

Telecom bills arrive every two months, and they should be paid promptly, or you risk being disconnected. About a year ago, I received a refund cheque from France Telecom, for 18F. This was unusual, but I accepted it without question. When paying a bill some months later, I enclosed their cheque, countersigned it, and sent it off with my cheque for the total amount less 18F. Three weeks later I received a letter telling me that unless I paid the 18F I had deducted from the bill, the telephone would be cut off. Why would they not accept their own cheque? It became a matter of principle. I telephoned the local telecom agency, and was put through to the Service Contentieux (complaints), obviously a very useful and very busy service, for it took some time. The conversation went as follows:

Me: I'm having a problem with the bill...

Man: (Wearily) Madame – everybody, everybody in the world has a problem with their bill. (Big sigh) You can't pay – is that it? (Small sigh).

This was *weltschmerz* touchingly personified. However, when I explained he told me France Telecom never accepted their own cheques in part payment. The deductions from that are somewhat disconcerting. Events were even more so ... my telephone was cut off because of the delay, even though I had paid all but 18F. The reconnection charge was £26, and I had to have a new number, which I still cannot remember. So much for principle!

Since January 1992 France Telecom has reduced its charges by 18 per cent for all very long-distance calls (USA, Australia, Hong Kong etc.), and by 13 per cent for most others. To all EEC countries charges are 50p per minute, peak time (Monday to Friday, 9.30 p.m. to 8.00 a.m.), and 39p off-peak (2.00 p.m. on Saturday to 8.00 a.m. on Monday).

France Telecom is capable of other surprises too. One month after receiving notification of this reduction of charges I was sent what I thought was another bill, only a week after the last. My hands were shaking with angry anticipation as I ripped open the envelope. This had to be yet another confusion. However *colère* finally dissolved into smiles when I read the missive. It looked exactly like a normal *facture*, but the bottom line of the last column told me that I had *un avoir de*, in this case 100F. I couldn't believe my eyes. I read and re-read; and even looked up *avoir* to check that it didn't have an opposite meaning. But no... it was actually a credit. In any case the box usually inscribed with the figures of the sum to pay was full of crosses. Could it be kisses from France Telecom? Another bouquet arrived from them last week. Once again a lowering of charges, and once again *un avoir de*, but much larger this time, and even more kisses in the right-hand box. If only British Telecom were similarly inclined.

If you wish to have a detailed bill (*facturation detaillée*) it will cost you 90p per month. The details given are date, destination, time of call, duration of call and cost. Very useful if you have friends who suddenly wish to call the office. And even more useful for holiday tenants. France Telecom have numerous services which are particularly good for holidaymakers who must keep in touch with the UK. For example, you don't need to own an answering machine if you are expecting an urgent call and have to be elsewhere. With very little notice, the operator will transfer your call to whatever number you give her. The monthly charge for this service is about £1.85. Not as efficient as an answering machine, but a convenient temporary expedient.

Insurance

For my five-roomed village house, with large roof terrace and bathroom, the annual multi-risk, buildings-only insurance is 416F. The minimum value for which you can insure furniture is 40000F, which costs about 300F per annum. My ground floor consists of a large vaulted garage. As there is no visible access to the living areas on the first and second floors insurance against burglary is not so essential. An outside staircase would certainly be an invitation to a passing *voleur*, and in that case an extra insurance would be wise.

Towns have a regular police force, but villages usually have one person of good standing to act as *gardien champêtre*, whose function seems to be surveillance and keeping the place tidy. Our *gardien* is a genial plasterer in his fifties who takes over the mayor's twice-weekly surgery up at the Mairie from time to time. He is built like a tank, so he would certainly give any miscreant a run for his money. It is as important as any insurance to leave the house key with someone. Good neighbours are the surest defence against house damage in any form, but more of that *entente cordiale* later.

If you do have to make a claim as a result of criminal damage, don't forget to report it to the police first. If it is not reported, the insurance company could well dismiss the claim. If there is damage to the house not caused by a criminal act, look up your local *hussier*, rather like a bailiff, ask him or her to inspect the damage and write a confirmatory report, called a *constat*. *Hussiers* are local VIPs, and the best allies in cases of claims and damages. Some friends, residents, bought a house which was in what they believed to be a state of completed renovation until the first winter, when a bitter north wind blew gallons of rain through windows and roof, ruining the new kitchen. Their *hussier* has enabled them to make claims, a year on, against the vendor, and they are succeeding.

Rates and Taxes

Rates are paid annually, and in both town and country consist of two parts. The *taxe d'habitation* is payable by the occupier, whether or not he or she is the owner. The *taxe foncière*, land tax, is paid by the owner. In 1991 for my village house I paid 950F *taxe d'habitation*, and 918F *taxe foncière*.

There have been rumours that the French government intends to introduce a poll tax system. As a result there have been even louder rumours concerning a second revolution. In my village alone there is open talk of barricades. I sincerely hope that the government will reflect on the UK's track record in this area before any decision is made.

As in the UK there is regional variation in these community charges. They are assessed by the Commune, the Departement and the Région. Much depends on the value of the location and on local amenities. For example, a public swimming pool will cost residents a little more. Where there is a local industry which pays tax (*professionel*) at a higher rate than the private householder (*particulier*), the tax paid by the local inhabitants will be less. So if you want to live in a remote village with swimming pool, sauna, daily rubbish clearance and a cinema, you will pay more than you would in, say, Arras, near the industrial estate.

Taxe d'habitation and *taxe foncière* are paid by the householder at the beginning of the year. When you sell up and move house in the UK, the solicitor usually tots up the proportion of municipal or local taxes due to your purchaser, and any reimbursements due to you. In France, you will have paid for the whole year, and it is up to you to make any just claim against the purchaser. Conversely, if you are buying, expect a bill from the vendor within a month or two.

Rubbish Collection

Poubelle (refuse) collection is generally made twice-weekly. In town in summer it is made daily. A few years ago any object could be left outside the door and it would be collected. This was an invaluable service, particularly when one was moving in or moving out. It does not happen any more. If the object cannot be squeezed into the large blue plastic *poubelle* bag (obtainable from the supermarket), it must be taken to the nearest dump. These are always to be found well outside village or town boundaries.

Some isolated hamlets do not have a *poubelle* collection. Our first house was in such a hamlet, and taking rubbish to the dump, a few kilometres away, was always the least favourite task. The tracks to the dump were so narrow and bumpy that you could guarantee the car boot would be awash with left-overs, vegetable peelings, lumps of garlic and fruit well past the eat-by date. A few weeks of this, and the aroma usually impregnated the car until Christmas. I remember having to be quite firm with my youngest child when I discovered she had been saving all the left-overs in a secret plastic bag to take back home to Sophie, our labrador, a blonde dustbin on legs.

One very good feature of the *poubelle* collectors is their efficiency. Nothing is left behind. There are no litter-strewn streets – the refuse collectors' calling-cards in my neck of the UK.

Paying bills

Make absolutely sure that the authorities who send you bills have your correct UK address. Paying can be a problem, particularly when you are given ten days to pay and the bill has taken ten days to reach you. Needless to say, the bills should be paid immediately if you wish to avoid the service being cut off. Even if it has the correct address, the French computer can sometimes make mistakes. For example, I used to live in the London area N1 8EH. The EDF regularly addressed their bill to N18, and forgot the EH. Perhaps it's a ploy to persuade us all to pay by direct debit, *prélèvement*. I have not yet had the courage to do that, because I never know precisely what is in the account, or whether cheques issued have all been paid in, despite reasonably regular statements from my bank in France. Officially, an *étranger* cannot be overdrawn. I was, once – never again – but more of that later.

EDF and GDF bills are paid to a Paris Cedex zip code, France Telecom to a large regional agency, and water charges to a local centre. All addresses are clearly marked on the bills. Should you change your UK address, obviously the authorities need to be notified. I have moved house several times over the past 20 years, and for the majority of those years I merely crossed out my old address, and wrote in the new one where indicated on the bill. Sometimes I have sent a covering letter. This has not been the correct procedure for some years, it seems: you are now required to notify the local agency – telephone number and address in the top left-hand corner of the bill – of any change of address. If they are sent to main offices, Paris or regional, any alterations or letters are thrown out either by the computer or by office personnel. But the good news is that local offices will take changes of address by telephone, and any problems relating to payment can be communicated directly to them – and are most courteously dealt with too.

Getting There

Finding the region and the house is one thing, but making the journey there is another. How you do it is generally a question of the available cash, especially with children. With almost limitless permutations of route and road, it need never be a chore, although with young children a plentiful supply of *divertissements* for hands and stomachs is essential. Pillows too, if you have the space – one should always travel in hope. A car is undoubtedly the cheapest form of transport for a family. Besides, once you start taking household paraphernalia down to *chez vous*, to say nothing of family luggage, there is no other form of transport that could accommodate the load. In the early years we were so loaded to the gunwales that wing mirrors afforded the only area of rear vision. My children have frequently suggested that I should buy an articulated lorry. Motoring down, I always aim for the earliest morning crossing, to make up for the hour we lose. The early crossings are, of course, cheaper, whether by boat, hover or cat. I personally prefer the latter, and not just for speed. The smell of bacon and chips on a boisterous sea is not my body's idea of a good time. Besides, it takes the edge off that first breakfast of steaming coffee and hot croissants.

One year, when the children were very young, and our dormobile finally gave up the ghost, we were obliged to leave it in the village while we returned home by train. At Avignon station, before we had even started, an elderly *voleur* snatched my handbag containing all our money and passports. My 11-year-old bravely gave chase, and with help it was retrieved. When we arrived in Calais, all hovercraft flights had been cancelled because the sea was too rough. Along with a horde of stranded passengers from previous flights, we were herded on to a very full ferry. It was Grace Darling weather, and the chances of clinging to the mast were slim. Consequently I spent the entire voyage alone, below decks, lying prone on a stone floor, wishing for death – as, I might add, were many others.

Finally we cast anchor. As the ship rocked gently from side to side, those of us below decks staggered up to the disembarkation point, where a large silent crowd had assembled, waiting for the 'off'. The force-ten gale had trebled crossing time, and it was small wonder the crowd was silent after a six-hour battering. I had no idea where my family was, nor did I particularly care. As I stood there, head down, praying for *terra firma*, suddenly loud shrill trebles rang out, piercing the silence and turning every head in my direction. 'Mummy! Mummy! Yoohoo... we're here!' 'Daddy says you've been sea-sick.' 'Are you still sea-sick, Mummy...are you?'

'Have you been very, very sick?' 'How much sick have you been Mummy...?'

Not the most memorable 24 hours.

Your house may be near enough to the coast to make the journey in one day, and if you have someone to share the driving, so much the better. My house is a ten-hour drive from the Normandy coast – that is, ten hours non-stop. I usually drive alone, so a comfortable night en route is essential. I do not consider this an indulgence. After all, it is likely that I shall be up to the armpits in paint, attacking a wall with a power drill ere long, so why not live superbly for one night? When the children were young we were obliged to find the cheapest possible *pensions*. So long as the place was clean, and there was hot water, a good meal was always assured. We also booked well in advance, an essential in the summer, and we were rarely disappointed.

The recent introduction of Formula One hotels is a godsend to families, as one room can accommodate a family of four. They are very clean, cheap (130F per room in 1993), and functionally comfortable. The ones I have used have all been very quiet and well organised. Senior citizen friends of mine use them regularly. The breakfast is copious enough to satisfy the most ravenous teenager. All Formula One hotels are situated just off the autoroutes, and if you cannot get a list from the French Tourist Office, try the ports.

Without the daily financial demands of a growing family, I frequently stay in rather more interesting places now. There are a number of glorious *châteaux* scattered throughout France, where for the cost of a night in a two- or three-star hotel, you can drift back into history instead. Smaller, blue-blooded versions of the *Guide Michelin* in booklet form, which list bed-and-breakfast *châteaux*, are available from good French newsagents.

Autoroutes are generally the most convenient and quickest means of travelling anywhere by car. However, in the past few years many RN (*route nationale*) roads have been enlarged into excellent dual carriageways, an improvement on the standard three-lane system, which is never easy with a right-hand drive car. And, of course, they're free. In the summer of 1991, autoroute charges from Calais to Avignon totalled approximately £40. Not so bad for a carload, but for one or two people a more significant expense – and you still have to return. The new dual RN routes are well marked in the latest Michelin maps, so it is worth abandoning those tattered, dog-eared folders stuffed in your car-door pocket and buying a new set.

Of course, you will not necessarily always be *en famille* when you visit your house. In the early stages, one person may need to make a flying solo visit to inspect the work, or pay the workforce. For one person it is very uneconomic to travel by car, unless you are within an easy distance of the north coast. Further away, car travel for the solo driver will only pay off if the vehicle is loaded with your UK surplus, and it saves hiring a van. Even so, hours of driving both ways leave little time to unwind in the middle.

Air France, British Airways and Air UK do fly-drive travel from London to most of the main French city centres. Although packaged, it is not cheap. The TGV (*train grand vitesse*), is always fast, comfortable, competitively priced and cheaper at certain times of the day. Paris to Nîmes takes only four hours, so if you took an early train or flight to Paris, you could arrive at almost any destination in France within the day.

Car hire in France is so wickedly expensive that it is cheaper to use occasional taxis, or better still, to have friends who will meet you at the station or airport and give you a lift to the supermarket when required. In the autumn of 1991, I tried another route, flying to Barcelona with a very cheap but comfortable, and reputable, fortnightly charter flight. I hired a Spanish car – small, but in perfect working order – for one third of the cost in France. This arrangement would suit anyone who has a house south or south-east of Toulouse, and who does not object to a drive. As a rough guide, Barcelona to Montpellier takes approximately three hours on the motorway. Unfortunately, the airport at Gerona, even nearer to the French border, closes in October every year. This route is well worth repeating.

Here's one that is not. One summer, with a very packed car, I started my journey from south Wales at 2.00 a.m. The roads were empty, and the driving effortless, as was the crossing. Breakfast in Arras took longer than usual because I was feeling somewhat limp after such an early start. Several stops for forty winks, and countless cups of coffee later, I dined at seven o'clock in a motorway Routiers restaurant, arriving at the house, the shopping done, at 9.15 p.m. After a chat and a cuppa with my neighbours, I unpacked, finally leaping into bed at 1.00 a.m. By now I was well into my third wind, and on quite a high at the prospect of doing it again next time.

I do not remember much about the following 36 hours. They were, to all intents and purposes, lost. Friends to whom I subsequently told the story of the marathon, asked, 'What were you trying to prove?' How right they were. Never again.

Food

There is always a temptation to cram a large box of food into the car, at least there was in our family, in the early days of house-owning. I do not think our minds had quite switched on to the fact that we were not going to a bed-and-breakfast where we would have to stock up for days on the beach, but to our own corner of a foreign field, where we could buy and cook as we pleased. Gradually, as the tins of beans and spaghetti multiplied and gathered dust on the shelf, reality took over. This was not a three-week trek, or camp, this was our home from home.

There used to be a few grocery items that were cheaper to bring from home, like soap, Earl Grey tea and good margarine, but nowadays France is generally better, not only for quantity and choice, but for quality, and at very competitive prices. The only reason for taking any foodstuffs there is either a larder surplus at home, a need for instant consumption the moment you arrive, or just personal preference. I always keep three items stocked up from the UK: muesli and cornflakes, because proprietary brands are slightly cheaper; Assam tea, not always readily available in French supermarkets; and Coffeemate, because it is creamier than the local variety.

In those early years we could seldom afford to buy red meat and doing without it became a habit that has grown into a choice. Chicken and spicy garlic sausages were favourites, and still are. We lived on salads, vegetables – a large ratatouille lasted days – cheese, fruit and yoghurt. Economy did not extend to *pâtisseries* and gateaux either, but tummies have never been flatter and firmer, and as a family we were never so healthy. Which proves the point, even today, that good simple food is cheaper in France.

I still have a guilty twinge whenever I succumb to a cake or a bar of chocolate. Purse strings condition like a Pavlovian dog. As supermarkets do not close until 8.00 or 9.00 p.m., it is ideal, we have found, to arrive in time to do a shop en route to the house. The next day may then be devoted to those dozens of jobs awaiting your attention; calling up the workforce, or just playing house, enjoying the sun and *chez vous*.

It is always possible to live in a village, however small and remote, without a car, bus or shop, and continue to eat. Approximately three times a week, visiting tradespeople, vans stacked with goodies, arrive in the village centre. And you will never miss them. Kilometres before they can be spotted, a very long, very strong blast on a klaxon bellows across the terrain. Depending on the merchandise, this can cause quite a flurry of excitement.

Matrons of all ages, shapes and sizes, retired old men, some with their dogs, lone dogs, foreign visitors and children run out of houses, tumble down stairways, appear out of dark alleyways, chattering loudly. They greet each other like long-lost friends, although they could be next-door neighbours, and gather round the van, transformed into a market stall, exchanging jokes and banter with the aproned knight. In my present village, we have a *boulangerie*, so there is no visiting baker. Henri, our *boulanger*, has a district-wide reputation for his excellent bread, which he bakes in a wood-burning oven. This enables the bread to be kept for a little longer, although I have no idea why.

Anyone wishing to know when the butcher is due only has to stroll into the village square and wait for the dogs to arrive. It is quite uncanny, but they are always there minutes in advance, trotting quietly into line alongside the van's resting place, and wait patiently with comportment and dignity (apart from a spot of undignified salivating) until the klaxon is heard.

The first holiday in *chez vous* is always exciting and intriguing. In every way it is a voyage of discovery. It may well try the patience of a saint at times, especially if you have moved into a *ruine*. But playing at Swiss Family Robinson for a week or two can be quite exhilarating and fun. Always remember, if you are planning for future improvement, it can only get better...and better.

Chapter Two

The Plan of Attack

If you have four walls, a roof, one solid floor and running water, you have the basic necessities for a summer camp. A spring camp can be a disaster. We made our first big mistake in our first house by assuming that March, south of Lyons, would be as balmy as an English summer. It was so bitterly cold that we had to put the camp beds together at one end of the large kitchen-dining room in order to share the heat from one electric fire and a fan heater. We had no hot water heating at that point, and a cold shower, although it was working, was out of the question. Strip washes were *de rigueur*, and undertaken, sitting in the shower tray, with a bowl of hot water. By late afternoon the temperature in our communal room began to rise, and by nightfall we would retire to bed in a roseate haze induced by good wine and good food. The mornings were quite the reverse, requiring all the enthusiasm and ra-ra of a girl guide camp to expose even one toe to the savage elements.

We had a dormobile at the time, so I had brought down all immediate necessities in several large boxes, plus a couple of surplus shelving units for the kitchen. I cannot remember what we managed to achieve apart from paying the builder and arranging the next stage of work. Nevertheless it was fun, playing house in another country. Everything was new, and so had we been, to the whole business of converting a *ruine*. We had gratefully taken advice, never questioning it. We were told we would have to have an architect, and were introduced to one. He assured us we needed him to apply for planning permission to turn the hovel into a *domicile*, and to make a roof terrace, which we had decided was to be a priority – the *raison d'être* for a place in the sun, as far as we were concerned. It was not going to be a straightforward exercise, as a new floor would have to be laid, wall to wall, in order to create a second-floor terrace, and then part of the roof could be taken off. But no problem, because he, our architect, knew a plumber, an electrician, a builder and a carpenter for the window frames and shutters. He would use his own colleagues. He gave us no choice. No comparative *devis* (estimates) for us, but at the time we were pleased to have the strain of searching, and the strain of language, taken from us. In retrospect, I would never take on such a primitive *ruine* again, and would strongly advise anyone contemplating such an undertaking to reconsider.

Although our 'architect' turned out to be a moonlighting surveyor for the local town council, he was assiduous in his supervision of the works, and kept the hamlet's elders happy with the changes being wrought in their midst. This was 20 years ago, and there had been little or no change here for a century. The hamlet consisted of one short hill, flanked by houses, most of them smallholdings with land at the back. Our house was at the bottom of the hill, and was part of the farm buildings, next to the chicken house. We had no land attached, hence the importance of a terrace.

There were no windows, merely two very large open squares, the size of doorways, on the first floor at the front, where grain and hay would have been hauled through. On the ground floor there were only slits in the two-foot thick back wall, wide enough to poke a rifle through. The inhabitants of the hamlet, an old Protestant stronghold, would have made use of these vantage points to pop any straying Catholics, and to defend themselves. Across the narrow road, my neighbour's family had lived in the same house for generations, and in her garden stood two cypresses signifying a Protestant burial place. The family's headstones dated back to the Protestant persecutions of the 17th century.

As we preferred light to the advantages of a rifle-range at the back, we naïvely set about measuring up for window frames. The land at the back belonged to Madame, next door. It was derelict, wild and used for nothing, not even her livestock. This was our first introduction to the Napoleonic Code, but we were bound to come across the good fellow sooner or later.

Up to this time, the only knowledge I had of the Code came from productions of *A Streetcar Named Desire* and Stanley Kowalski's rantings, which did not apply to Madame and her land. Certainly no Blanche Dubois, Madame, known as the 'Poisoner of the Village', was not a bundle of laughs. The Code, as the architect/surveyor explained, forbids windows overlooking another's land, lest rubbish be tipped out. With a sympathetic neighbour a mutually acceptable arrangement could have been made. It is now the law in France that in such circumstances a window for light only may be inserted into a wall, provided that the glass used is opaque enough for the neighbours to have high jinks on the overlooked terrain without being gazed upon, and identified presumably. The window should not open – back to the rubbish again – but an air brick may provide ventilation.

Had this been the case 20 years ago, there would have been no need to confront the most disliked woman in the Commune. Although I doubted my chances of even being given an audience,

I girded my loins one morning, and knocked on her large wooden door. After several minutes, I heard the flapping of sandals on stone. Bolts were released, and the door's hinges groaned into action. There stood the Poisoner. She was under five feet, very broad, dressed from head to toe in black, and held the end of a long rope in her hand. At the other end of the rope stood a tall goat, sporting a jaunty straw hat. The surprisingly large courtyard was full of flowers, in pots and in hanging baskets, and displayed banks of thick blossom. Her house, looming large and impressive behind her, had two sweeping stone staircases to the living quarters.

She stood quite still, daring me to speak. I asked politely, stuttering and stumbling over French grammar. She waited. I finished, and I waited. I thought, hoped, she would have a change of heart, after all, the weeds on her patch were as high as our gun turrets. It was at this moment that the tall goat, with consummate elegance, strolled over, and stood behind his mistress. They made a charming couple. For the briefest of moments she considered my request for three tiny windows in place of the slits on the ground floor. Then she took a deep breath.

'*Non!*' she snapped.

Then, the goat, snapping his mandibles in sympathy, as if to endorse his mistress's decision, began to bite off, and instantly consume, every sunflower head in the bed behind her. Should I say something? Shoo the goat away? The visual effect was mesmeric.

Oblivious to the background scene, Madame continued: '*Absolument non! Non! Non!*' and slammed the door. For the next four years after that, I barely saw her. As for the goat, I never saw him again. However, the builder did chip away at the gun slits sufficiently to make little windows, two and a half feet by two feet, installed quietly during an afternoon zizz time in mid-August.

I had another problem with a window, or rather, the lack of a window, in my present house, overlooking someone else's patch of land. The windowless room was potentially a single bedroom, placed between the bathroom and double bedroom, and in the house's heyday would have been a dressing room. The patch of land in question is untidy scrub, unused, on which stands an open-ended shack, straddling the width of the patch. I have heard it called a garage, but collapsed carport would be more accurate. It is owned, as is the house across the square, by a centenarian, who now lives with her family in the nearest large town. The house is visited from time to time by her disagreeable grandson and his current belle. The patch of land is never used, its tall iron gates never opened.

When I bought the house, I was told by the vendors that the owners of the patch had agreed to the insertion of a window in this wall. So my builder went to see them at their town flat for formal permission. He was refused. They expressed a wish to see me, which eventually they did. I was given permission for a window with opaque panes of glass. Permission for a small ventilation pane was refused. Did they imagine I would stuff pieces of decaying vegetables through the mini-louvres? As the projected window was to be above the carport roof, they gave permission for the builder to stand on his ladder on their terrain when necessary. Materials were bought, and the date fixed for hacking out the aperture from the inside. It was to be a metre square. Suddenly, just before my departure, I received a telephone call withdrawing permission, with a few lame excuses. Alice, the octogenerian mum of my closest and dearest neighbours, dislikes this family with a passion.

'*Paysans!*' She spits out the word. '*Ils sont que paysans!*'

Although the neighbours insisted I had the law on my side,

the builder, Dominique, was hesitant to go ahead, particularly as I would be absent. I was therefore despatched forthwith to see Monsieur Bruno, the mayor. He was angered at this *volte face* as it clearly contravened the law. We were to go ahead, with his blessing – let them dare oppose!

The window is now successfully in place, with a ventilation brick at floor level. So take heart if you are facing a similar problem.

When we built the terrace in our first house, the same problem, overlooking Madame the Poisoner's land, pertained. We had managed to insinuate the small windows, but the law, 20 years ago, relating to terraces was different from present-day requirements. The wall directly overlooking her land was of the regulation height, one metre. A second wall, one metre high, had to be constructed half a metre inside the original. It was suggested that we left the second wall standing for a year, then took it down, brick by brick, which, of course, we did. So much for red tape.

In the town house, some ten years later, I had another terrace created from a room at the top, this time overlooking my own courtyard. It did not cross my mind that I should need planning permission until my neighbour, a charming Parisian, whose holiday home was the mansion of the district, and sported a plaque commemorating Richelieu's visit in 1628, explained that as we were in a conservation area, permission was necessary. He must have seen my look of despair.

'Don't worry', he smiled. 'I shall say nothing, but, perhaps you would be kind enough to add another half-metre to your terrace wall. Hmm?' His balustraded stone staircase, fit for any Romeo, backed on to my house, and obviously he did not wish to be seen tripping down to breakfast in his dressing-gown. He could see us, too, but we had assumed that he had a sort of territorial *droit de seigneur* as we were living in a retainer's hovel which would have slotted neatly into his courtyard with room to spare. So of course we were kind enough. We were in no position to argue.

Planning Permission

Planning permission for alterations to a *domicile* are dealt with either by the mayor or by the local municipal authority. For changes which do not affect the general aspect of the house, it is the mayor who gives permission. For more significant changes, permission is given by the local authority. The procedure for the latter is similar to that of the UK although less bureaucratic. Not knowing which permission would be necessary for my present terrace, taking off the front part of the attic roof, yet again, and building up the wall to the regulation height, I first went to the Mairie. With help I filled out a form.

Two weeks later I was told to supply photographs of the façade, and three copies of a drawing showing how the proposed alterations would affect the aspect, plus three copies of a plan of the terrace. An architect friend suggested I made a drawing from a photograph adding a couple of sun umbrellas where once the roof had been. I took them in to the municipal planning department personally, and talked to the man in charge. Because there was to be no significant alteration he was perfectly happy for the work to be carried out. It was up to the mayor to decide. Monsieur Bruno did so the next day.

As for the side wall which overlooks the carport terrain, the law has changed again. The wall in question has to be 1.80m high, with a return of 60cm. The other two walls, overlooking the square and a narrow alley, are the regulation height, one metre.

It is not worth trying to beat the authorities and going it alone. Somebody somewhere will complain about debris, dust and scaffolding, and there is no comeback without permission, only aggravation.

Conservation Areas

Before you start thinking about painting the outside shutters and window frames, find out if you are in a conservation area. If so, your paint colours will be restricted. In my town we had a choice of grey, brown, or a delightful eau de nil, which was very attractive against the cream stone houses.

One advantage of a conservation area for the householder is the availability of grants. Our town was, overnight practically, given prominence by the French government. They designated it a town of historical significance, and not before time. This meant that money for refurbishment was available in the form of generous government grants. Within a year the changes wrought were remarkable. The grubby façades of the mediaeval quarters were sandblasted into a glorious cream stone. In the poorer areas, where houses huddled together around public edifices, the differences were very noticeable. Rotting *volets* were replaced, woodwork was repainted, and developers turned huge, decaying 15th-century mansions into luxury apartments. With mouldings, architraves, arches and doorways cleaned and preserved to perfection, it was like suddenly stepping back into the Renaissance.

It is strictly against the regulations to tamper in any way with these stunning façades, and that includes the insertion of a roof terrace. However, I have seen examples of the only way to overcome this problem, bearing in mind that access to fresh air is very necessary in town during a long hot summer. A room at the top has the roof, from the sloping section, removed. The façade wall remains as before, room height, as do side walls. With no roof the floor has to be waterproofed, and tiled, as for a *bona fide* terrace. What the flatholder has, as a result, is an enclosed terrace – no guaranteed suntrap, but certainly cooler than anywhere else in the house. It is the price exacted for living in such period elegance for the rest of the year.

From the time of its historical recognition the town became '*recherché*', and has never looked back. Property leaped in price, and has remained more or less at that level. The owners of poorer properties, with no bathrooms, and no central heating, muscled in on the new value of their *domiciles*, and had their much-needed improvements paid for. Although my house had been in the right quarter for a grant, when my builder explained the laborious process of application, plus the obligatory services of an architect, I lost interest. For a permanent home, it would have been worthwhile, but time was against applying for anything. In any case, government money, whether in the UK or in France, is not given without a few strings attached, and I did not wish to have any restrictions placed upon me and my holiday home, other than taxes, bills, and putting the rubbish out on the right day. But that was my choice, and each to his own. If you have a house in an historic location, it would be worthwhile finding out about grants.

Plumbing

France is a constant delight and surprise, and that includes her plumbing. It used to be, and to a degree still is, a standard joke with some Brits, rather like the mother-in-law. Jolly hilarious squatting over a hole in the ground, what? Like going native! Despite the fact that modern French plumbing is excellent, and highly sophisticated, this super-sophistication is frequently juxtaposed with turn-of-the-century primitive. In Avignon a few years ago, I saw, and used, the first of those circular street loos that look like a telephone box. A few yards away was a brasserie with a rather smelly hole in the ground. Naturally, being in town, both would have been on main drainage – *tout à l'égout*.

However, even if your village is on *tout à l'égout*, your house may not be. In which case it will be necessary to dig a *branchement*, a link pipe to the street drain. That, of course, means replumbing the system, which in most instances is no mere embellishment, but a dire necessity. Our first house – I use the term loosely – had no water, and the village no *tout à l'égout*. Eventually water was piped in, and the only way to take anything out was through a septic tank (*fosse septique*). Our architect/surveyor knew exactly which type to buy for us – I presumed there was a choice of shape, size, colour? It would be placed under the window in the projected shower room at ground level. The loo was to be placed immediately above on the first floor, for technical reasons. We were assured there were no problems, we should leave it all to him. And why not, we thought? After all he was collecting his ten per cent from us and, probably, from them. No matter, we should be returning to a house instead of a pile of stone. Just before leaving I met the plumber, a small intense man with glasses, who carefully wrote down all the basic requirements, shower, loo, washbasin, in his neat pocketbook. We went through a price list, looked at photographs, made the choices. Just as we were about to shake hands, until the next time, he suddenly looked at me, wide-eyed, his eyebrows touching his hairline:

'The bidet, Madame – you have forgotten the bidet!'

He smiled, took out his pocketbook again.

I had remembered the bidet. I wanted to forget the bidet. Why couldn't he? The plumbing was already costing more than the budget, and it did seem a little like gilding the lily to have a bidet, and no mains drainage. The two did not go together. But there was something about the look he gave me when he sensed my hesitation.

'Surely,' he insisted, 'Madame will have a bidet – surely?'

My spirits cringed. I felt unclean, unwashed, unhygienic, a thoroughly disgusting example of a British upbringing. There was no defence against the innocent purity of this Gallic accusation. In two seconds I had capitulated. We would have a bidet.

We were pleased with the plumbing, particularly when the hot water system was installed. The shower worked well, the loo flushed magnificently – but the *fosse septique* was a nightmare. It was the size of a deep, open coffin. Family burial vault would have been more accurate. The size was of no importance, as there was plenty of room for it under the window. It was the smell. At first, unused as we were to septic tanks, we thought the smell was normal. It was when we saw our usually polite, charming neighbours hold their noses as they walked past the house that we realised something was amiss.

Our *fosse* was the conversation piece of every pastis party we held. It was the major topic of conversation at every other gathering in the village. Everybody gave us advice. We were told to buy a special disinfectant powder. This we did, by the kilo, to absolutely no effect. Smells would emanate from this burial chamber whenever the loo was flushed, even without the loo having been used. I went through so many cans of air freshener, it is quite possible that our *fosse* was responsible for the first snick in the ozone layer.

The shower room itself became a haven for local wildlife. From time to time a mouse would skate across the damp tiles and take five for a pirouette before scuttling into a hole. After a week or so, no one screamed any more. We, the mice and us, accepted each other. Scorpions were different. It was easy to see their black shapes on the plaster. Getting into the shower was like a scene out of *Psycho*. You never knew what you might find. The bidet had its back to the *fosse*, another hazard. Heaven knows what lurked in those pipes. One night, as I was about to use the bidet – well, we had it, so why not? – I saw a long, black rodent tail disappear into the *fosse*'s pipe. All this and the smell too!

After dozens of telephone calls, our self-styled architect's plumber, a different one this time, erected a tall tin chimney with a pointed cap on the terrace. It looked as if it had been taken off a Romany caravan. We were assured this would do the trick. The result was worse. Not only did the shower room continue to smell, but suddenly, in the middle of a sunny siesta on the terrace, depending on the prevailing breeze, a pungent aroma of boiled onions assailed the nostrils. Why boiled onions we never knew, but assumed it was a combination of *fosse* and Ambre Solaire.

Fortunately for our wellbeing it was possible to keep our living area upstairs and the downstairs bedrooms free of smell by closing doors, so we were still able to entertain our friends and neighbours. It was the street that suffered most. At any time I was prepared for a bell-ringing hamlet crier to shout 'Unclean, Unclean' from our doorway. The *fosse* was ours. It reflected us, and worse still, appeared to display our appalling digestive systems. Making dignified exits and entrances was not easy. The village treated our *fosse* problems sympathetically, but in such a small community, our *fosse* was their *fosse*.

Meanwhile we continued a barrage of angry telephone calls to the surveyor, who seemed never to be at home. Each time a neighbour strolled past the house, there would be a loud verbal explosion of shock-horror, and a firm grasp of both nostrils between thumb and forefinger. We took to using loos in restaurants and cafés as frequently as possible. At the end of that first holiday season in our new home we had decided that something drastic had to be done. It was the *fosse* or us.

A couple of days before returning to the UK, my husband fell victim to a touch of Montezuma's Revenge. At 4.00 a.m. he staggered out of bed, said he couldn't possibly use our loo – think of the *fosse*, think of the children, think of the village – whereupon he donned his dressing-gown and slippers, and walked out of the house like Captain Oates of the Midi, to find a quiet patch of a foreign field, preferably with plenty of cover. This was not difficult, as we were surrounded by dense shrubbery, trees and *garrigue*. Dawn was just breaking, the village was silent. He found a suitably concealed clearing, proceeded to descend groundward in a crouching position, ready to obey natural impulses, when a deafening salvo blasted forth, from within touching distance. A moment of silence, then a frantic rustling in the bushes surrounding him. About ten men, some of whom he knew, emerged from their camouflage, brandishing shotguns, hip flasks, and bottles of wine. Nothing was better designed to put a bung in Nature. In a flash he had rearranged his garments and, whistling nonchalantly, attempted to create the impression that he was merely taking a sunrise stroll. The men were as surprised as he.

'Bonjour Monsieur' was followed by a round of shaking

hands, introductions, and the pressing of liberal quantities of alcohol down the early-morning whistler's throat. Had Monsieur forgotten, this was the first day of the *chasse*? Monsieur had certainly forgotten.

We returned to the UK, and mains drainage, with gratitude, but our *fosse* and its effect upon village life and possibly by now upon the surrounding flora and fauna was never out of mind. It was a complete surprise when we returned late in the following spring to find the village street inaccessible. There were barriers across the pot-holed country lane which, over a distance of 50 yards, became the one street. We parked and investigated. Our arrival was clocked within minutes by Charlot, Emile and Fernand, three middle-aged brothers, our opposite neighbours, who greeted us with the best news since Ghent communicated with Aix. The *fosse* had created such a problem, even unused, throughout the winter that a deputation, consisting of almost the entire village – the total population numbered 12 – met the mayor of the Commune to complain. He came along to sniff the air, and a decision was made. The village was to have *tout à l'égout*.

Each household was obliged to pay, but no one minded. The three brothers had visited Paris two years previously, and had been awestruck when they saw no dirty water running alongside the pavements, to say nothing of the sanitary arrangements. From that time they were sold on *tout à l'égout*. All smiles, they admitted that our *fosse* had done the trick. A few days later, when the sewage pipe was cemented over, the village, and in particular, our family, pulled its chains with triumphant abandon. The cost for us was 2500F, and worth every centime.

Electrics

In older houses, you usually find that rewiring is necessary. Even if you are acquainted with electrical installation, as either a DIYer or a professional, think several times before you attempt it. The EDF inspect, as do our Electricity Boards, and if you are not a French electrician, there could be problems. In any case I have been told that the new EDF regulations are far tougher than ours. Extensions to an approved system are different. I know of several British residents who have extended their own power and light. If the house is to be rewired, you will be asked how much power you would like. The average small household, mine included, generally receives 6kw of power. For this, the standing charge is 30.20F per month. Of course, you may want more, in which case the charge increases. In UK households, power depends on a variety of factors, not least the capacity of the local sub-station. However, for the purposes of comparison, the average load is not likely to exceed 3kw at any time, according to the electricity board.

For a holiday home I, personally, do not think it is worth that extra expense. I have managed for years with 6kw, and the only time the supply proves troublesome is in winter when I overload the system. Generally, amending this simply means turning something off and resetting a fuse switch or two. But there was one occasion when it was not quite so simple. The weather was bitterly cold I recall, and I was using, simultaneously, the washing machine, electric kettle, electric toaster, oil-filled electric radiator, two fan heaters, house lights and a couple of lamps.

The heating problem was temporary – my plumber was girding his loins and workforce to install the oil central heating. Meanwhile, the weighty overloading on this particular evening plunged the house into complete darkness. Fortunately, I knew where the candles and matches were kept – always know where they are. The fuse board switches were all, surprisingly, on as they should have been, but the EDF's *conjoncteur* told a different story. The red button was in the 'off' position, depressed, while the black button had popped out, signifying that the supply was off, and refused to budge.

After half an hour of unsuccessfully trying the old tricks, I rang the electrician, who attempted to tell me what to do. I realise he must have found me exasperating, because electricity and I are worlds apart even in English. In French, his excitement mounting with each misunderstood instruction, it became very trying for both parties.

Finally, with an audible gulp of some essential lubrication, slowly and with extreme vocal control, using not only my first name – we were on first name terms – but my surname too, he commanded that I should listen and obey. He made himself very clear, and like an admonished pupil I followed instructions, which worked. Just in case anyone else has the same problem, the procedure is as follows:

1. Switch all the fuses to 'off'.
2. Push in the black button on the *conjoncteur* box. The red one will now pop out.
3. One by one, switch on the fuses. This way you will discover the rogue final straw.

At least this should save having to call up the electrician, and lose house points. And if a 6kw *puissance* is insufficient for your family 9kw will cost a 97.3F per month standing charge, and 12kw will be 137F, plus TVA at 5½ per cent.

New wiring will require a new meter. If the meter is housed

in a box on the outside wall of the house, you pay more for the installation. On the other hand, you benefit from correct readings. Most of us make do with internal meters, and either leave a key with a neighbour so that the EDF can take an official reading, or wait for a major readjustment on a later bill, when either you take a reading yourself, or are in time to pick up the meter reader's card in your letterbox. In any case, it is always a good idea to read all meters before locking up the house.

Plugs

A word here about plugs for those who are not quite *au fait*. A *prise du terre* is, as its name suggests, a two-pin wall socket with a protruding earth pin. For smaller electrical items – iron, hairdryer, lamps – a small simple-to-wire, two-pin plug is all the apparatus requires. For more powerful appliances – electric kettle, washing machine, toaster, fan heater – you will need the larger plug, two pins plus a channel for the socket's earth pin. When wiring, if you observe the UK system, i.e. brown wire to the right, and blue wire to the left of the earth channel, you won't fuse the circuit. At least I haven't yet.

Central Heating

Let's face it, central heating is a luxury in a holiday home, because usually the house is used only in the warmer months of the year. Certainly for anywhere south of Lyons, central heating is last on the list of priorities. This does not mean it is unnecessary, *au contraire*, but you won't need it as often as in more northern areas. It has taken me 20 years to have a central heating system installed, and I have done so for several reasons. As time goes on I should like to spend more time at the house, without being confined to the summer. We are told that Christmas dinner is usually eaten outside in shirtsleeves. Certainly, I have sat at café tables basking in the sun in late November, but it is from January to the beginning of April that the real winter sets in. These months are particularly attractive if you are near enough to ski centres, which makes ski weekends possible and cost-effective. There are plenty of small ski resorts dotted around France that you will not find in travel agents' brochures, and generally both downhill and cross-country skiing are catered for.

Using electric fires and fan heaters all day is very expensive, even in France where power is cheaper. Another advantage of a centrally-heated house, wherever it is in France, is the possibility of winter lets. At least it keeps the house aired, and it helps a little towards the next season's expenses.

If you live in town, and have town gas, then gas central heating is the cheapest to run. Installing the system is, like oil (*mazout/fuel*) expensive. If you live in the country and favour gas, it has to be bottled. You need land to house the enormous containers, not a pretty sight. They are very economic to run, but again quite expensive to install. Oil is, as everywhere, dependent upon world markets. It is running neck and neck with gas at the moment. Electric central heating, with off-peak radiators, is very reasonable to run, and certainly the cheapest to install. I would have liked this system, but was dissuaded by the electrician and the plumber. Apparently, the insulation in old houses, especially if the rooms are quite large, is so poor that it can reduce the heat output by as much as 50 per cent. This does not apply to new houses, where electric central heating is the most popular form.

Many country *domiciles* use wood-burning stoves to centrally heat, provide water, and often to cook with, depending on the type of apparatus. The fuel is frequently free, or so it appears, for weekly excursions into the countryside foraging for wood becomes a way of life for some families. My neighbour Eli has built a long, low-slung trailer for the sole purpose of collecting logs. The whine of his electric saw is heard for days after a haul. I cannot think that all the logs are for use in his small house, but there they are in his workshop, packed tightly together leaving barely enough room for a pair of feet. Beaming, he explains he is now ready for the ice cap and a polar winter. He says this every year.

Purchased wood is sold by the ton in my part of France and cut to any length, but I have been told of a curious standard of measurement which relates to the length of a man's arm. Should you come across this old tradition, make sure you have a de Gaulle with you and not a Napoleon.

Whilst the sight and aroma of burning logs is evocative of peace and comfort, the thought of how many trees may have to be massacred to provide just one village with enough fuel for a week teases the conscience. I shall stay with subterranean fuel.

The central heating *devis* for an oil system in the next chapter will give some idea of the expenditure required. But, quite frankly, for average purses it is not an essential at the outset.

Chapter Three

Finding the Workforce

I have been propositioned by more French builders, plumbers and labourers than I care to count. Please do not assume that I am some sort of beauty or sex symbol. *Au contraire!* – I am a well-into-middle-age, very average mum, but French men are above all gallant, and it is their attitude to women that puts them strides ahead of the average British male. And this attitude goes across the board, from artisans to professionals.

When I was signing the papers for the purchase of my last house, there we were in the *notaire*'s office, the estate agent, the *notaire*, his partner and his assistant. I was the only woman. The conversation was light-hearted and joky. They were charming, courteous, and declared how good it was, now, to see so many women in the business world. I said I should be very surprised to hear such sentiments expressed by a similar group of British men. The estate agent, an urbane Parisian, smiled and said, 'But you see, Madame, we French, we actually like women – *like* them – you know. That is the big difference.' True, but of course there are other differences:

1. To the average Frenchman, a woman's age is quite irrelevant. This is always flattering.

2. It seems to offend his masculinity to see a woman coping

alone with the complexities of electrics, plumbing, plastering and cement. To say nothing of having to fetch and carry, often to excess.

3.   He is protective of women in those areas designated as a 'man's' domain.

Traditional, old-fashioned, maybe, but never underestimate the influence of Maman and his wife. Naturally, his Gallic gallantry does not bat an eyelid when his wife waits on him hand and foot at home, particularly if she is a *femme de foyer*, a housewife. Before feminist gorges rise, let me assure you that she, Madame, is the clever one. No home maintenance for her, thank you. I seem to remember that, in the 1960s, when we were fighting every inch of the way for the women's movement, Germaine Greer and feminism, we were happily applying ourselves to all kinds of house maintenance to prove a point. And in many families, mine included, if the wife did not do the DIY, it was never done. But, alas, we had the wife, mother and wage-earner roles to play in addition. By the 1970s we were beginning to feel the strain. At the time we thought French women were slower to catch on, slower to emancipate themselves. But were they, are they? After all, female emancipation is only relative to the male's attitude. In the French homes I know, the *poussin* and the *perceuse*, the *moules* and *marteau*, are kept quite separate.

The advantages to be gained from this status quo by we foreign DIY females are legion. Imagine the scene: a hot steamy afternoon, builders are tapping round the house. You, clad in shirt and shorts (not too short, and a bikini is going too far), perspiration running down your face, dislodging a lump or two of mascara, are trying to tighten a screw into a wall bracket. You have successfully plugged the wall, but have ruined the screw head by using the wrong-sized screwdriver, thus having either made the groove twice as wide, or flattened it completely.

As you sigh and swear in English, the builder comes by. He throws up his hands in amazement, at both what you are doing and how you are doing it. He gives you a friendly, but patronising little smile, shaking his head from side to side, tut-tutting the while. He peers carefully at the screw, examining it. You bemoan the poor quality of the metal. He shakes his head again, and inspects your screwdriver. More tutting. Then, from his tool bag, he brings out the present his wife (clever again) gave him for Christmas: a battery operated, fool-proof, fail-proof automatic screwdriver. He either does the job for you in five seconds flat, to a suitable accompaniment of your '*mercis*', or, better, he will tell you to run along, repose in the sun, and leave it for him to do later.

Let me give you an example. In our first house – in the old days when I did not take DIY too seriously – I was trying to plug a 400-year-old rock face with a hand drill. It was having about as much effect as an egg beater. However, after what seemed like hours, one bracket was in place, not very securely, and I was grinding my way into the second when a neighbour dropped by. He was appalled, both at my archaic drill and the lack of a spirit level, as I was putting up a shelf. No tut-tutting, but very raised eyebrows, a loud high-pitched whistle, and his right hand waggling stern disapproval. He motioned me to stop. In a moment he was back with his power drill and level. Twenty minutes later my shelf was up, firm and straight. It is insulting to offer neighbours payment, but a long cool drink on the terrace was certainly in order and much appreciated.

But back to propositions from the French workforce. The following illustrations are solely for the female reader, and any male with a passing curiosity about the *modus operandi* of certain French artisans. The first step is to ask you to '*tutoyer*' him (use the familiar form of 'you'). Unless you want to, i.e. if he looks like Warren Beatty/Mel Gibson/your particular favourite, decline this invitation. Should you agree, the next step is to ask whether he may '*tutoyer*' you. From this point, be assured, it is a downhill struggle, but of course, it all depends on him.

About ten years ago, I was in dire straits trying to cope with the mildewed results of a flood which had occurred in my absence. A friend sent along a builder who, unbeknownst to me, was having trouble at home. I used to wonder why he was happy to work until nearly midnight, plastering in one room, while I painted in another. The work was scheduled to take about a week. He was easy to get along with, worked very hard and did not drink, so we regularly consumed quantities of coffee, tea and sometimes supper. After a few days he was playing romantic cassettes. In a week he was telling me what he would like to do to the house, repairs, reconstructions. He was right. He had good ideas, but I could not afford the cost of this concentrated onslaught, and told him so. The next day, he told me, quite seriously, that he would like to turn my house into a beautiful little doll's house. He would do everything for me, paint, build a new kitchen, and I would never have to lift a screwdriver again. Heady stuff, and very appealing. But the cost? No cost at all – he would simply move in! He was soon put right on that point..

At the end of that working holiday I was preparing to leave the house at 4.00 a.m. in order to be in London by nightfall. He had been given the keys, and jobs left to do had been discussed and finalised. Getting up at 3.00 a.m. is never advisable because no matter how much self-discipline is exercised it is almost impossible to have an early night beforehand when you are packing up the house. At 3.30 a.m., barely awake, I was groping with what felt like a croissant and a cup of coffee when the bell rang. It was the builder. He had come to say goodbye. Now this was indeed a novel experience for me.

As I was attempting to steer the croissant in the general direction of my mouth, with varying degrees of success, conversation was limited. How had he managed to leave hearth, home and marital bed at such an hour? Simple. He had told his wife he was going out to collect snails. Try that one in SW11!

Another proposition, though less forceful than the builder's, came from a plumber. He had seen the work required of him, priced it, and had kindly thrown in a hand washbasin. As he was taking his leave, he clasped both my hands in his, and in a voice trembling with emotion and pungent shock-waves of concentrated garlic, he said: 'They tell me you are all alone, Madame. How difficult it must be for you, how lonely...Let me help you, please? I could visit you...often. Please, I would like that so much...' I wrenched my hand from his sandpaper palms, and explained that much as I admired his sentiments and sensitivity, I could never entertain the idea of taking him away from his wife in the evenings, lest she should be lonely, too. Why didn't they both come over to see me for an *apéritif*? The subject was never mentioned again. A far more genteel approach, nevertheless, than 'Come 'ere doll'.

So much for propositions, now back to the workforce. There are dozens of self-styled 'artisans', and finding the right combinations for you can be a lottery. No matter how much you try to eliminate the risk factor, you cannot win them all. Many times in the past when I thought I had made the right decision, mistakes, ranging from minor to catastrophic, occurred. But had I been advised, been told who to ask, errors would have been minimal. It is vital to find artisans who are trustworthy, and able to work more or less to your specifications in your absence. A poor workforce at home is infuriating, but at least there is frequent supervision, and appropriate action can be taken if necessary. A poor workforce in France induces insomnia, for there is little one can do save withholding whatever payments are outstanding. And we all know the cost of righting wrongs.

Finding the Right People

The first step towards finding your workforce is to ask the people from whom you bought the house, and the estate agent. He will certainly know of artisans, but for the sake of self-protection may decline to recommend. The *boulangerie*, particularly in a village, is the community's nerve centre, a hotline to everybody and any alterations/renovations taking place within a sizeable radius. Ask around in cafés, bars, restaurants, *tabacs*. Better still ask your neighbours, and look through the local freebie paper, which usually has a whole page of plumbers, electricians and builders. Within 48 hours you should have a paper list of artisans sufficient to rebuild the entire neighbourhood. If you are not personally acquainted with any Brits in the area, the estate agent will probably know a sprinkling. They would be worth contacting, as recommendation is the very best advertisement, although not all compatriots are necessarily helpful. If they have found a team of treasures, they may wish to keep them for themselves. It is as well to bear in mind that prices charged to the British are usually higher than those the locals expect to pay, so check out any estimates with your neighbours.

If at this point you have still not found a satisfactory team, go to the Mairie, as all qualified artisans living in the Commune are registered there. Had I known this many years ago, and checked out the Mairie's list, one particular cowboy would have been conspicuous by his absence. The Mairie also has an annually-updated average cost of works. For example, all building work, including masonry, plumbing and electrical work, is costed by the square metre or metre. This is essentially a guide only, and not to be taken too literally. My plumber tells me that plumbing costs on the list are higher than his. Much depends upon the amount of work being done, the easy – or not – accessibility of the site, and of course the personal contact, which is a major factor. As soon as you have your shortlist, and before you start asking for *devis* (estimates), it is very important that you try to see the work of the people you have chosen. Even if you cannot find examples with your neighbours or friends, almost all the builders I know have built their own houses, so invite yourself along. You will generally find a modern villa, often with a porticoed verandah. Some would be more at home on a *Dallas* set, with ultra-stylish, ultra-modern fitted kitchens and impeccably tiled floors. Do not be put off if the surrounding terrain resembles a builder's yard, it usually is one.

When we bought our first house in France, it was little more than a hole in the wall. To be precise it had been a *mangerie*, a *bergerie* and *grenier*, with oak-fronted, zinc-lined cattle troughs, still in place, all along one wall on the ground floor, and a very large, very high-ceilinged granary, plus a smaller room, on the first floor. The stone staircase would have been perfect for the Scottish play. After the first season, having just about achieved a basic standard of living, with hot water, plumbing of sorts, and a roof terrace with fabulous views, the next step was to erect a staircase from the kitchen-diner to the large skylight opening on to the terrace. The children were young and seeing the ladder sway each time they romped up and down to the roof was unnerving. Downstairs we had one bedroom, a bathroom and a large open space. We wanted a dividing wall built to make two further bedrooms out of the space, keeping the troughs as dressing-tables and suitcase repositories.

We were putting off the problem of finding a builder to do this. Then, one morning, my husband returned to the house full of joy. Not only had he found a Spaniard in the local bar (he loved the Spanish language – his was good, and he found French impossible), but the Spaniard was also a builder, and was coming over to see us. And so Juan arrived. A tall, lean, dishevelled man, with a black stubbly chin and loud rasping laugh. When he spoke French his accent was so thick that he might as well have been speaking Spanish, so all discussions took place in Spanish. My husband was delighted at this opportunity to air the language, but this may have been where it all went wrong. Juan came over to see us with his sons, nice lads, and his wife, a quiet hard-working lady who spoke very little French. We went to see them in the house that Juan built, which should have told me something, but 20 years ago I thought anyone who could build a house had to be some kind of latter-day Nash.

And so it came to pass that Juan started work for us. He would arrive any time between 10.00 a.m. and 11.00 a.m., always smiling and amiable. At noon, he would be off for his *déjeuner*, returning at two, still smiling, even more amiable, and swaying. At six it was down tools for the day, followed by a long *bavarde* in Spanish with my husband, with a bottle or three of red plonk. How he ever made it home, I shall never know. At seven, eight or nine, he would stagger to his car, a clapped-out Citroën, rev up the engine furiously in clouds of exhaust, and attempt to drive up the five-foot wide steep incline that served as the hamlet's street, disappearing like a bat in bumper car. We would clap hands over ears, and shut eyes when he took off. He became so unreliable that we called him 'Juan day he's here, Juan day he's not'. He became a family joke, or perhaps a salaried court jester would have been more accurate.

At last the *cloisons* were built, quite satisfactorily, and we had bedrooms. We left the house keys with him to build the staircase. Very carefully, I drew what we wanted. The staircase was to be fixed to the floor, have a *main courante* (banister), look as though it had always been there, and above all safe. He understood that, didn't he have children of his own? Instructions were given in French, Spanish and sign language.

Something in his interpretation must have been lacking that day. We returned to Juan's staircase. It was little more than an ugly, unplaned, bulky stepladder. It was not secured, and stayed in position by sheer weight, the top step leaning against the skylight frame. There was no *main courante*. Surprisingly, there were no mishaps to friends and family for the several years we remained in the house. Aesthetically it was a disaster, and you could guarantee a splinter or two with each ascent.

After our initial shock, the neighbours recounted how the thing had been built. It had taken two very drunken afternoons, a few days before our arrival. There was no redress. He had an answer to everything. We rid ourselves of Juan, but had to live with his monstrosity for ten years. Needless to add, he was never on the Mairie's list.

The *Devis*

Reading and understanding the *devis* (estimate) is bad enough in English. In French it is awesome, so have a dictionary handy. It took me years to realise that to *pose* a washbasin, or lavatory, means simply to fix it in position. On some *devis* you find the extra words *mise en service*, which means to connect up and leave in working order. If these words are not added it does not necessarily mean your loo will be left solely as a conversation piece. Only if the word *fourniture* is included will the article be supplied. So if you expect the whole exercise, article and function to be supplied, plumbed and/or working, look for: *'Fourniture et posé*, on the *devis*, but always check that it will be left in working order, just in case semantics happens to be your artisan's hobby.

Over a period of two years an averagely good builder worked for me. *Devis* were read, accepted, work done and paid for. Some weeks after the last piece of work had been completed, I received, to my surprise, a gigantic bill from a builders' merchant, for sand, cement, plaster, bricks, nails, screws, filler – you name it, it was listed. Naturally, I thought there had been some mistake. But no. The bill covered the years he had worked at the house. It seems I had been paying only for his labour. As he is still on the loose, and there may be others like him, I would suggest that all potential clients check this out when agreeing to a *devis*. You could end up paying for screwdrivers, lunches and overalls! My mistake again. This builder was not on the Mairie's list, and I hope he is never likely to be.

Whenever possible, I prefer to scour around for fittings and fixtures myself, unless it happens to be a specialised object like a hot water tank. Certainly, second-hand kitchen and bathroom equipment is readily available (See Chapter Five).

Examples of Recent *Devis*

Figure 1 is a *devis* for central heating (...and don't think you will never need it).

Figure 1

DEVIS: FOURNITURE ET POSE CHAUFFAGE CENTRAL		
MATERIEL:		
1 chaudière fonte DE DIETRICH chauffage seul	Ff	11.806,00
68 éléments de radiateurs fonte aluminium à 95F pièce	Ff	6.460,00
7 robinets thermostatiques à 150F pièce	Ff	1.050,00
7 coudes de réglages à 60F pièce	Ff	420,00
1 cuve à fuel 2000 litres	Ff	3.600,00
TOTAL HT	Ff	23.336,00
TVA 18,60%	Ff	4.340,49
TOTAL TTC	Ff	27.676,49

Figure 2 was my plumber's estimate for central heating materials some 18 months ago. I could not afford to pay for the installation as well, so my plumber suggested I just buy the materials, which he would then store, as prices were rising all the time. This he did, although I shall never know whether he used mine and bought

Figure 2

INSTALLATION		
EQUIPMENT – POSE – MISE EN SERVICE:		
1 chaudière + 1 cuve à fuel	Ff	1.500,00
7 radiateurs à 3.000F pièce	Ff	21.000,00
TOTAL HT	Ff	22.500,00
TVA 18,60%	Ff	4.185,00
TOTAL TTC	Ff	26.685,00

more for me this year when the system was installed. It matters not, but I did appreciate his labour charges remaining the same even after nearly two years.

The total in sterling comes to about £4,500HT. My house is large, the rooms vary from 15 feet by 17 feet to 12 feet square and the ceilings are high, so I do not think I would have fared better in the UK. The plumber has taken great care with the system and has made good everywhere, even going as far as repainting a corner of a bedroom wall.

When I moved into my present house, the water had been cut off, and there was no hot water system, save through the coal-fired *chaudière*, a Rayburn lookalike, circa 1930, in the kitchen. There was, and remains, a beautiful cast-iron tub bath, and an Edwardian washbasin. The loo was a most elaborate affair, with no flushing water and consequently no cistern. Instead, a delicate lever at the side, when raised, tipped the zinc floor of the pan, allowing everything, including the obligatory bucket of water, to be flushed away. The trouble was we were never quite sure where, as there was, at that time, no *tout à l'égout*. I have kept this old artefact, just in case there is ever a remake of *Murder on the Orient Express*. The kitchen sink was not much later than the original, which would have been installed when the house was built, in 1815. It is grey stone, large and shallow, tucked away into a type of corner dresser, with one tap. During our first summer, we stood a bowl in it for washing and washing up. When it was emptied, water ran straight down into the garage below, and thence out into the square. As personal washing habits became a public spectacle, we began to experiment with the sweeter-smelling washing powders and liquids. Anything to offset the smell of stale water hanging about the front door. And we certainly did not want a repetition of the *fosse septique* saga. With the tap removed, the sink is now part of a shelf unit.

Figure 3 is the plumber's *devis* for the removal of the old system, and installation of the new, including the *tout à l'égout branchement*.

If there is anything in this *devis* you do not understand, take the dictionary from the bookshelf and start looking up now.

The electrical state of my present house was deplorable, if not dangerous. The kitchen walls were festooned with black cables, the wires laid bare in places. The electrician removed the old system free of charge, and naturally it was not in his brief to make good that part. Consequently I have used quantities of filler in the dozens of lacerations and craters left behind. I remember watching, fascinated, while the electrician's mate, a huge lad, not too bright, and nicknamed '*La Bête*' by the others because of his inordinate strength, ripped, pulled and dug out every piece of the old wiring. He appeared to be enjoying himself hugely, laughing, and talking to

Figure 3

DEVIS: INSTALLATION SANITAIRE		
DEPOSE ANCIENNE INSTALLATION	Ff	1.500,00
EQUIPEMENT – POSE ET MISE EN SERVICE DE:		
1 WC, 3 lavabos, 1 baignoire, 1 évier,		
2 machines à laver, 1 cumulus à 500F l'un	Ff	4.500,00
DEPLACEMENT DE LA CUISINIERE	Ff	1.800,00
BRANCHEMENT AU TOUT A L'EGOUT:		
5m de tranchée dans le béton et sur la route	Ff	2.000,00
ECOULEMENT DES APPAREILS EN PVC:		
10m PVC Ø 100 à 140F le m posé	Ff	1.400,00
5m PVC Ø 63 à 130F le m posé	Ff	650,00
10m PVC Ø 40 à 110F le m posé	Ff	1.100,00
ALIMENTATION GENERALE EAU FROIDE		
DU COMPTEUR JUSQU'A L'EVIER		
10m PENAFLEX à 60F le m posé	Ff	600,00
ALIMENTATION EC/EF EN TUBES CUIVRE		
env. 60m de cuivre à 90F le m posé	Ff	5.400,00
1 CUMULUS ELECTRIQUE 200 litres	Ff	2.000,00
TOTAL TRAVAUX HT	Ff	20.950,00
TVA 18,60%	Ff	3.896,70
TOTAL TRAVAUX TTC	Ff	24.846,70

no one in particular, while quantities of even older wall cascaded over him in large lumps.

The electrician hoped I had not decorated, because he warned me that the new installation was going to be messy and damage the wall surface, but of course he would make good. He was right. *La Bête* applied himself with even more strength and vigour as he drilled and gouged out deep channels traversing each wall for the new cables. It was a chaotic week of noise, grit and drilling, particularly as the plumber was doing his bit as well. To be fair, they asked me to leave, not that I had insulted them, but presumably they could have piled up the debris with even more abandon had I been elsewhere. But I remained at my post. There was nowhere else to go, and nowhere escaped the dust and plaster, not even the loo.

That was another story, and another complication. The bathroom door had to be removed for the purposes of plumbing, thus exposing loo-users not only to the army *in situ*, but also to any prying villager who happened to be at an upstairs window at the time. Curiously, the workforce seemed never to use it, although whenever I was obliged to shuffle past the open space, I averted my gaze, coughed, and broke into song, just to be on the safe side. However, as Frenchmen tend to use the rear wheels of their cars as mobile *pissoirs* on motorways with ne'er a shrub for cover, I feel sure my modesty was unnecessary. In any case, the two hours for *déjeuner* gave the lads a fighting chance to sort out their systems. Mine suffered untold privations, particularly as the force arrived for work at 7.30 a.m. Consequently I had an arrangement with my neighbour.

Towards the end of that egg-bound week, the plumber announced that the new loo was ready to be installed. The *tout à l'égout* had been dug, piped and cemented, and the old contraption disconnected. It gave me quite a frisson of excitement, the thought of flushing water at last. The moment arrived. We all gathered around the new loo, as for a birth, and stood in reverential silence, while the plumber played midwife. Although the loo was in position, my excitement was short-lived. There could be no flushing until the next day, for a reason known only to the plumber. He must have seen my disappointment. Before he left he filled four very large buckets of water, and arranged them neatly round the new loo. 'There, Madame,' he said, 'they should keep you going until morning.' There was enough water to keep half the village going all night.

Figure 4 is part of the electrician's *devis*, straightforward and quite typical. If you are likely to be reading one similar, make sure you understand everything. For example, a *télérupteur* is not someone who talks all the way through 'Panorama'.

Last year I was able to give the go-ahead to my builder for the terrace project in my present house. The front half of the *grenier*'s roof was to be taken off, the existing floor transformed into a flat roof with cement and ceramic tiles, and a wall, the regulation height, constructed all round. I read the *devis* carefully, as I did not want a catastrophic repetition of the last terrace. If half the *grenier*'s roof is removed, something has to be done with the other half. At some point in the future, it will be another bedroom, but for the moment, rather than build a dividing wall, we decided to put in a large window. At least it is a small start. You have to be able to reach a roof terrace, so I supplied a self-assembly staircase. My builder fitted it, and supplied a landing, hand rail and outside door for the terrace, strong enough to withstand the rigours of a Provençal winter.

Figure 5 is the *devis* for the major works and **Figure 6** is the *devis* for the attendant extras.

It was when I was about to settle up these bills, after all the work was complete, that the shock came. After all these years, and after all the *devis* I have read, mistakes can still be made. Perhaps not so much mistakes as omissions which, if not questioned, are not

Figure 4

DEVIS ESTIMATIF

CUISINE

1 télérupteur, 3 poussoirs pour 1 centre	Ff	760,00
3 groupes de 2 prises avec terres	Ff	1.260,00
1 prise 32 Amp avec terre (four)	Ff	740,00

SALON

1 va et vient pour 4 appliqués	Ff	1.120,00
3 groupes de 2 prises	Ff	1.260,00
1 simple allumage pour 1 lamp sur terrasse	Ff	410,00

CHAMBRE 1

1 télérupteur, 3 poussoirs pour 1 appliqué	Ff	760,00
3 groupes de 2 prises avec terres	Ff	1.260,00
1 ligne sur lavabo avec réglette comprise	Ff	580,00

BAINS

1 va et vient pour 1 centre	Ff	520,00
1 ligne sur lavabo avec réglette comprise	Ff	580,00
1 prise avec terre	Ff	300,00

PETITE CHAMBRE 2

1 va et vient pour 1 appliqué	Ff	520,00
3 groupes de 2 prises avec terres	Ff	840,00

CHAMBRE 3

1 télérupteur, 3 poussoirs pour 1 appliqué	Ff	760,00
2 groupes de 2 prises avec terres	Ff	840,00

DEUXIEME ETAGE

1 va et vient pour 1 appliqué	Ff	520,00
1 boîte de réservation avec 1 ligne lumière et 1 ligne prise	Ff	1.280,00

VERRANDA

1 télérupteur, 3 poussoirs pour 2 appliqués	Ff	880,00
2 groupes de 2 prises avec terres	Ff	840,00

ESCALIER

1 va et vient pour 1 appliqué	Ff	520,00

Figure 5

DEVIS DE MACONNERIE

Dépose complète de la toiture et descente des matériaux.

	m2 55 à 110,00F	Ff	6.050,00

Dalle béton armé avec ancrage périphérique et toutes
suggestions d'étaiement et forme de pente

	m2 2,4 à 3.650,00F	Ff	8.760,00

Enduits à 3 couches sur murs pierres

	m2 60 à 160,00F	Ff	9.600,00

Reprise de rives sur toiture restante

	ml 10 à 190,00F	Ff	1.900,00

Pose et fourniture de carrelage en grès spécial terrasse

	m2 40 à 270,00F	Ff	10.800,00

Arrase des murs pierres périphériques de la terrasse

	ml 32 à 105,00F	Ff	3.360,00

Location grue ou lève matériaux

	Estimé:	Ff	4.000,00

	HORS TAXES:	Ff	44.470,00
	TVA 18,60%	Ff	8.271,42
	TOTAL TTC	Ff	52.741,42

CONDITIONS DE REGLEMENT:

    1/3 à la commande
    1/3 en cours de travaux
    le solde à la fin des travaux

BON POUR ACCORD

DATE

SIGNATURE

Figure 6

DEVIS DE MACONNERIE

Maçonnerie d'agglos de 17,5 en mur périphérique sur arrasse		
m2 16,22 à 280,00F	Ff	4.541,60
Fourniture porte pleine 200 x 80, selon catalogue		
LAPEYRE, bois exotique no 334	Ff	2.500,00
Maçonnerie en sous-oeuvre pour cette porte,		
comprise scellement	Ff	2.400,00
Fourniture d'une fenêtre 100 x 80		/
Maçonnerie, enduit et scellement de cette fenêtre	Ff	2.500,00
Pose escalier, fourniture palier et main courante	Ff	2.200,00
Ouverture en sous-oeuvre dans chambre, et fermeture		
pavés de verre 80 x 80	Ff	4.500,00
Enduits à 3 couches sur maçonnerie d'agglos		
m2 20 à 160,00F	Ff	3.200,00
		————
	Ff	21.841,60
ARRONDI A	Ff	20.000,00
		════════
HORS TAXES:	Ff	20.000,00
TVA 18,60%	Ff	3.720,00
		————
TOTAL TTC	Ff	23.720,00
		════════

---

mentioned until after the event. It appeared I owed the plumber a further £2,000. For the terrace, with not a loo in sight? For the waterproofing. This is apparently the plumber's job. As the terrace is about 25 feet by 18, four *couches* for *etanchéité* totals a fair amount of materials and labour. Naturally, one cannot argue against the importance of rigorous waterproofing in so vulnerable an area. In my case I suppose I was, of necessity, blinded by science, but I do have a 20-year guarantee. So be warned, in advance, to make sure the waterproofing is accounted for.

My present house has a long glass lean-to conservatory along one wall, and opens on to a terrace. It is apparently a fairly typical turn-of-the-century addition to older village houses. The plaster on the inner wall of my conservatory was coming off in chunks, revealing the very attractive original stone wall. A builder agreed to hack off this crumbling plaster in time for my next visit. The hacking was indeed thorough, for he left the wall pitted, paper thin, and with as many holes as a piece of emmenthal. A 25-feet-by-20 wall, with a slight wobble and a door frame on the point of collapse, is no joke.

My neighbours were witness to the details of the massacre. The day before my expected arrival, the builder turned up at the house with two young lads. Armed with sledgehammers, the boys sweated and hacked all day, covering the entire village square in a layer of dust and creating noisy havoc. When the builder arrived in the early evening to pick them up, he obviously noticed holes where there was once wall. All hammering ceased, and there were sounds of loud admonishment, panic, and a frenzied clearing of dust and rubble.

Naturally, when I actually saw what they had done, I was furious, dismayed and depressed. The wall would have to be rebuilt, and I would have to find another builder, as the current one accepted no liability for the underlying structure, and I should end up paying for hacking services as well as any new work. It was cheaper to start again. It's an ill wind, for a Brit resident chum recommended the team I have used ever since. I call them the Three Musketeers, Dominique the builder, Jean-Claude the plumber and Daniel the electrician. They are not jacks-of-all-trades. They have their particular *métier* although they know enough about each other's skills to help out when necessary. Hitherto, I seem to have found builders who professed to know the lot. Beware: in the long run they are not cheaper because their competence is so often called to account. My team lived in different villages, and are therefore registered with different Mairies, but registered they are. They each have a couple of workmen, sometimes not up to standard, in which case they will work all hours to put right anything which has not been well done. These are the types of artisans absentee owners particularly should have. They take the pain out of long-distance supervision.

TVA

French VAT is 18.6 per cent, and is applied in much the same way as in the UK. Most artisans try to avoid it, or at least part of it. TVA usually adds that extra, intolerable amount to a *devis*, especially when you are struggling to update your *maison secondaire* on a tight budget. Strictly cash deals – *noir* – are negotiated frequently, depending naturally on the amount of work to be done, and the size of the enterprise carrying it out. The larger the contracting company, the less likelihood of an all-cash deal, and vice versa. If the artisan is having to buy materials, he will have to pay TVA, and will pass it on to you. Make sure you receive an invoiced account for this, which, in case of a possible house sale in the future, you must keep for Capital Gains Tax.

Capital Gains Tax

Should you sell up and take the sale money back to the UK, the CGT is payable there. My experience has been confined to selling and buying on in France and, all things considered, I have had very little to pay, largely because the houses I took on were near collapse at the outset. Don't worry, you will never have to pay CGT in both countries. Another piece of good news is that if you hang on to your *maison secondaire* for 30 years, there is no CGT to pay in France. As in the UK, this tax is calculated at 33.33 per cent of your profit, although when all the deductions for annual property value increases and all the expenditure invoices are made, the profit margin is usually considerably decreased. It is the lawyer negotiating your sale who calculates the differential for which you must supply invoices. He then works out your financial liability and submits his figures and your invoices to the relevant government department. It is he who must give the whole transaction his seal of approval, not the tax man. The tax is then deducted from profit, and the rest sent on to you. All this takes about as long as the 'completion' period of a house purchase in the UK.

I sold my last house to a young couple from Annecy, and I agreed to use their lawyer, primarily because it was a good excuse to visit that delightful town. Although I had sheaves of invoices I had not actually done my sums, nor put them in any kind of order. On a Saturday morning we actually completed the sale, but the lawyer could not begin the formalities until all tax requirements had been met. I spent the following two days in a mountain chalet overlooking the lake, knee-deep in bills, hoping and praying to balance profit and loss. I did, more or less, and by Monday morning everything was delivered to the lawyer's office, and the sale proceeded as normal. One day I plan to make a return visit to Annecy, and to actually see the town this time.

I have always felt that the tax is unfair on those of us who, to a greater or lesser extent, are keen *bricoleurs*. We spend hours beautifying our homes, hours of sweat and toil, and are finally penalised by having to pay tax on any profit which, to my mind, we justly deserve as recompense for hard labour. Would that governments saw it that way.

Some friends of mind found a neat solution. He is a retired surgeon, with incredible manual skills – fortunately, I daresay, for past patients. Over a period of about 15 years, he all but rebuilt, and completely redesigned, what started as a modest stone *remise*, transforming it into something approaching a keep or folly. It had several levels, with terraces, bathrooms, shower rooms, and mezzanine floors. He cut stones, he laid floors, he plastered, he built walls, he put in the electrics, and he plumbed, which I suppose says much for Edinburgh University's medical training. With enormous foresight, knowing his predilection for super *bricolage*, he had put the house in his wife's name. When they sold up two years ago, he was able to supply all the bills, in his name, for labour and materials. A scheme worth noting if you are similarly inclined.

Having discussed at some length the ways and means of finding a workforce in France, I shall recount another cautionary tale, one which had disastrous results. During the first August in my town house, I took over a couple of British builders. We hired a van into which we piled a bathroom suite, two washbasins, two loos, kitchen units, and two new divan beds. They agreed to work for a weekly sum, to be paid in francs, and I opened an account at the local builders' merchant. This meant they could simply point to materials in the yard, as they knew not a word of French. The house did already have one cold tap, and one outside loo. The builders agreed to put in a bathroom, washbasins in bedrooms and a shower and loo in the top floor attic. There was nothing here that they had not done before in the UK.

But I also wanted a roof terrace created from the attic floor's separate back room. This meant taking the roof off. I was assured there would be no problem. Lifting off the roof was easy, and they would simply waterproof the tiled floor. Were they the proper tiles, I asked? Again I was assured they were. At that point I left them to it, and returned to the UK.

I know they worked late, because I discovered that my neighbour, the urbane Parisian, had asked them to stop hammering at 10.00 p.m. Not that they had been working like slaves: unused to the sun, they had lain comatose with heat and wine each afternoon. However, they completed the work, and returned apparently disgruntled with the whole exercise. Not nearly as disgruntled as I became the following January.

I received a telephone call from friends to whom I had given the house key. There had been a spell of heavy rain, and purely out of interest, they had called at the house. On opening the front door, a putrid smell had assailed their noses. It came from upstairs. No *fosse septique* this time, but mould covering the main bedroom underneath the roof terrace. The ceiling and walls were covered in this evil-smelling slimy layer of black. Part of the ceiling was already down. The new divans, pillows, bed linen and blankets, black and rotting, had had to be thrown away. They managed to salvage a few pieces of soft furnishings, but very few. Even the floor rugs, again new, were jettisoned. My friends did what they could, and covered the terrace in a plastic sheet.

But unfortunately it was no real protection against fierce downpours. I returned in the spring, and found French builders to relay a waterproof terrace, as it should have been in the first place. As if that were not enough, I had to call in a French plumber to replumb both leaking washbasins. The moral of this unfortunate tale is always use local builders, particularly for something as important as a terrace. After all, they know the country, the climate and the building traditions. Ours, it seems, do not.

Damp

Habit and tradition are fundamental elements in building, and there are as many differences as there are national frontiers. While I would never ask a Briton to build another terrace in France, I do not think I would ask a French builder to put in a damp course in the UK. Not that they are incapable – far from it – just different. Horses for courses – damp ones. But maybe I am being old-fashioned, and the European Community will change everything. When I lived in my town house, the one with the British-made terrace, I had damp in the sitting room and kitchen, despite the large cave underneath. This was probably due to an old communal well, which sprang into life underneath the damp wall. Not only my French builder, but others to whom I spoke, had never heard of the hacking off plaster, injecting, coating, replastering technique. Perhaps this is a peculiarly British building feature? A skill developed as a result of our climate?

The French solution to damp, the one I was given, was a *cloison contre l'humidité*, a complete damp course. While this is totally effective, it is messier, and six inches of room space is lost to the *cloison*. Nevertheless, it works.

Agents

There are a number of British expatriates scattered throughout the popular regions of France who, for a fee, offer to collect and supervise a labour force for any work to be done. This may be attractive, but it is not necessarily a trouble-free system. Some friends of mine employed one such agent to find a plumber, in their absence, to put a washbasin in a downstairs cloakroom. Naturally, they wanted hot and cold taps fitted. All this was explained to the agent *in situ*. They returned to find a washbasin with cold water only. The agent's French had apparently not been good enough to explain clearly what was needed. Not a very serious error, and one that was put right, but some cannot.

A family I know of, having found their house, took up the offer of a British 'friend of a friend' to supervise the lot. Estimates were chosen, and they were asked to part with £30,000, to include the friend's fee. The house was large, potentially stunning, and in a state of disrepair. The new owners were busy, professional people and were happy to leave everything to their new acquaintance. After several months of waiting, and much correspondence, they made their first inspection visit. Nothing whatsoever had been done. Worse still, their £30,000, so the bank informed them, had sunk without trace in the 'friend's' bumper overdraft, and needless to add, so had he. They are still looking for him. Be warned. Be on your guard.

In the experience of many householders, the more you are able to supervise personally, especially in the initial stages, the better. At least until you know the measure of your workforce. It's a long time from September to April, and if you are having major changes made, it is worth a flying visit, even if only to keep the lads on their toes. If you are a keen DIYer, the bulk of house refinements will probably coincide with family holidays. The temptation is to rush at jobs to get them done, as I did, but for the sake of the family, particularly if they are young, spread the work. You have time and there will be plenty more holidays. For several years in the first house, I seemed to do nothing but DIY, which naturally irritated the children. There I'd be in wellies, up to the elbows in cement, and there they'd be, wanting to be taken to the beach.

All it requires is a little planning, and everyone is happy.

Chapter Four

Settling In

Furniture, Floors and DIY

When it comes to furnishing the holiday home, most of us have the odd cupboard or table which could be transferred from the UK without leaving noticeable spaces behind. This is sensible and practical, particularly if you are able to transport smaller items in your car. If you happen to have a vanload of surplus furniture, it is worth taking it over, even when hiring a van, provided you are not planning a two-month sojourn. What doesn't pay off any more is buying new furniture in the UK to furnish the French home. The only largish items I brought from the UK at the outset were three chests of drawers, surplus to requirements there, and six specially purchased folding camp beds.

Customs

The attitude of customs officials to household appliances brought into France has changed considerably during the past 15 years. The fact that there is a growing number of Britons with French homes must have had an easing effect.

Fifteen years ago, when we decided to buy a larger dishwasher in the UK home, the obvious place for our old, dying table model was the French house. Unaware of any regulations, we were more than surprised to be stopped by the *douanes* at Calais. Admittedly, it was out of season, late at night, there were few cars passing through, and the boys were probably bored, but it took two hours before we could continue the journey. I have never seen so many heads poking their noses into one battered old dishwasher. No, we were not going to sell it – who would buy it anyway – yes, we would buy in France next time, and yes, it was for our new holiday home. Fortunately I had been advised to obtain a letter from the mayor of our Commune assuring whomsoever it may concern that we were the owners of a house, address, Commune and *cadastre* supplied. I should add that the last hour was most convivial, and ended with an hospitable flow of wine – duty free, I suppose.

This was the only occasion on which a proof of ownership letter has ever been asked for, but not the only time I have been questioned. About five years ago, on my return trip, I was grilled by a highly-suspicious woman customs officer at Dover. She wanted to know precisely where I had been, for how long, where the house was, how much of the year I spent there, and so it went on. Finally, she let slip the cause of this quizzing. It was my power drill, on display in the car boot. I had to work hard to convince her I personally used it for DIY. I think there had been a spate of bank robberies at the time, and clearly I looked a likely accomplice. With such eccentricities in attitude and questioning, I now always carry a house bill with my French chequebook, just in case proof is ever asked for.

On the other hand, I once brought back a tall walnut buffet in three parts. Shrouded in a blanket in the capacious car boot, it resembled two large coffins. As the car I had was not unlike a hearse in shape, I should have thought the combination was highly suspect, but not a question was asked.

The good news is that since 1 January 1993, controls have been lifted on goods entering France from another EEC country.

No duties are payable on used personal effects, household goods, old furniture and vehicles imported for personal use, providing the VAT has been paid in the country of purchase. Naturally there are some exceptions: drugs, firearms, weapons, threats to health and environment, etc. These are subject to prior authorisation from French customs. New household goods purchased free of tax – VAT – will be taxed in the country where they will be used, so with TVA at 18.6% in France, at the time of writing, you would be one per cent worse off.

Basic Furniture

There are certain basic items of furniture which the average family cannot do without. They are, in no particular order: beds, table, chairs, sink, cooker and refrigerator.

All these, and more, can be found in the competitively-priced *hypermarchés*, which are numerous: Carrefour, Conforama, But, Montlaur, Genty, Champion, Bazarland, Cora, Continent, Mammouth, Euroloisirs, Euromarché and Continent are but a few. They all spend a fair amount on advertising, and in a month you will have accumulated a formidable collection of pages offering special bargains in all those near you. Though names of *hypermarchés* vary from region to region, relatively few central managements hold all the strings. Near me is a massive *hypermarché*, which used to be called Euromarché, but is now Carrefour. Another started life as Montlaur, then became Genty, and is now Continent. If you can wait, don't rush into buying until you have combed the bargain pages. Here are some price examples of these essentials, taken from a cross-section at the time of writing: a sturdy metal-frame single bed base with 13 wooden slats (*sommier à lattes*): £25 (Euromarché),

£30 (Carrefour); similar with 26 slats: £50 (Conforama).

A mattress (*matelas*) will cost anything from £45, depending on quality. I would not recommend the thick foam variety. Comfortable they may be, but they are to be avoided in hot weather, unless you do not mind waking up sticky, and in a pool of perspiration. We have one, which we now relegate to the emergency spare. Beds with wooden sides and headboards, plus mattress, start at £105. Conforama usually has a good selection. For real economy you could buy French mattresses for UK camp beds, as we did. There will be time for replacement later.

You will find a wide variety of tables and chairs in the *hypermarchés*. We bought our very large pine table, and six 'Van Gogh' ladderback, rush-seated pine chairs for £38. But that was 20 years ago, before the birth of *hypermarchés*. New tables are quite expensive. The cheapest *pin massif* kitchen-diner table I have located was £100 in But. For better value tables, always try the second-hand market (see Chapter Five). When buying wooden furniture, look for the word *massif* in the description, because it signifies solid wood. Anything else is an agglomerate. *Massif* also applies to many other articles, particularly brass, copper and silver. So if you do not want a plated metal or a veneered chipboard, look for *massif*.

Chairs seem to be better buys. Conforama sells two *hêtre massif* (solid beech) Van Gogh chairs for £45, and a wide selection of other designs. Marble and wrought-iron bistro tables, though not suitable for large-scale entertaining, are very useful, attractive and excellent buys. I bought both mine, one for France and, later, one for my UK home, at Euroloisirs for £60 apiece. From the same place, bistro chairs in black, white or red are between £12 and £14, half the price of the same chairs in the UK.

When I moved to my present house, there was cold water only, and I kept the original shallow stone sink as a shelf, and built a shelving unit around it. I found a 100cm stainless steel sink, with mixer taps and waste fittings, plus a 100cm white two-door, one-shelf unit for £110 in Conforama. Always ask for special offers, even if you cannot see anything advertised. If you want a smart fitted kitchen, with cupboards top and bottom, you will find a selection ranging from melamine to solid oak (*chêne*) and pine (*pin massif*). For example, Conforama sells a white melamine ensemble for £290, consisting of the following: larger cupboard (200cm wide), four-drawer base cupboard, three-door base cupboard (120cm wide), top corner shelf unit, top single cupboard and top three-door cupboard(120cm).

I have never had money enough to spend on a super matching kitchen in my French holiday homes. That's the problem when one buys broken-down *ruines*. That is not to say that kitchen furniture and appliances should not attempt convenience; after all, the emphasis has to be on the holiday aspect of the house. This was never so apparent as in our first *ruine*. We had plumbing, sanitation, a cooker, refrigerator and very basic furniture. Returning home one hot afternoon, with a bootload of food shopping, I was beginning to feel the strain of all the hard, physical work we had been involved in during the previous weeks. We had laid a stone tile floor, roughly plastered a couple of walls, painted a large kitchen, and there was more to do. Already my biceps were aching from too much cement-mixing, although by way of compensation I had worked off excess from other parts that diet hadn't a hope of touching. Approaching the house, and looking forward to a long, cool drink on the terrace before preparing something simple to assuage appetites permanently on red alert, I espied two motorbikes parked outside. Inside, four large lads, whom I knew from the UK, were already into their umpteenth coffee with my teenage daughters.

So what was new? This was like old times. My pique was only too evident. For the next hour I was ushered into dark corners, by each of the girls in turn, as they expressed with total innocence their amazement at this unexpected invasion. I learned later that our guests had been invited at the end of term, albeit casually, but the young have a disarming habit of taking the casual literally, if it sounds a good deal.

Cooking for eight with only a sink and a card table was not my idea of holiday convenience, and with no spare cash, a DIY solution had to be found. Fortunately, I had always loved Lego, so a quantity of large oblong bricks, about two inches thick, was bought, and cemented together to form a honeycomb of deep shelves around my sink. Very *rustique* plastering followed, covering the new unit inside and out. On top of this construction an L-shaped section of melamine working top was fitted, cut to size at the local DIY shop.

To celebrate the birth of this family addition a village *apéritif* party was arranged – no big deal this, as there were only eight houses in all. I have never seen the local macho brigade laugh so much. Pierre, an ex-Legionnaire turned house renovator (his own), was crying into his pastis as he mumbled, '*Mon Dieu, c'est une danseuse espagnol – Mon Dieu!*' Then he slowly ran his finger down a perpendicular edge. The curve was only very slight, I thought. Fernand and Charlot, two farmers, tried to push it. They sat on it, leaned heavily against it, but it moved not. I was jubilant. The test flight had to be over. But not quite. Pierre placed his glass on the worktop, and asked me for my spirit level. Now, I had read about them, but at that stage in my DIY career, I had never actually *used* one let alone possessed one, and said so. That did it. They gathered in a sniggering silence around a collection of full glasses, placed purposefully on the unit. Fernand fetched his spirit level. We watched, and waited. There it was, irrefutable evidence. It sloped from stern to prow. The full glasses lent further proof. Never mind, it was solid, and the lads generously gave it a round of applause.

The next morning, early, Pierre arrived with several wooden wedges to straighten up the sloping top. After time spent muttering, filing and fitting, filling the house with cigarette smoke, and flamboyant use of a spirit level, perfection was achieved. *Entente cordiale* was more established than ever.

Cookers and Refrigerators

New cookers, particularly gas, are reasonably priced. For a holiday home I would choose gas rather than electricity, and bottled gas, if there is a choice. It is so much cheaper, and there is no standing service charge. Electric cookers will require a higher kilowattage than is normally supplied to small average households, consequently the standing service charge is higher (see Chapter Two). This applies equally to mixed cookers with gas hobs and electric ovens. Here are a few recent special offers:

Sidex	Gas, 4 burners, thermostatic oven	£110	But
Brandt	Gas, 4 burners	£149	Conforama
Fagor	Gas, 3 burners, thermostatic oven	£149	Conforama
Faure	Mixed, 4 gas burners, grill, thermostatic electric oven	£248	Conforama
Vedette	Gas, 4 burners, spit, autoclean oven	£360	Conforama

Indesit   Mixed, 3 gas burners, 1 electric,
          electric oven with spit   £248   Conforama

Microwave ovens start at about £110 with varying degrees of power and efficiency. For £185, you could buy a 1200w oven with grill. I do not possess a microwave in the UK, and I would not want one in the holiday home. For anyone setting up a future retirement home, however, a microwave could be a worthwhile investment.

A refrigerator is a must. Obviously, if you are going to have a new one at home, it makes good sense to put the old one in the boot the next time you make the journey south. All you will need is a change of plug.

I bought my *frigo* in France, a Philips, £70 from the local bankrupt stock shop. At the time I foolishly did not realise I would need a decent-sized freezer section. Ice cubes are a priority in hot weather and they take up far too much space in a mini compartment, which mine is. Weekly food markets are so tempting, and it saves holiday time and effort to buy as many main meals as possible at one fell swoop, and to freeze them until required. I have spent so many years cursing the paucity of freezing space that next season I shall visit the bankrupt shop again. Before you buy new always check out your nearest shop. Recent prices of new *frigos* include:

Indesit   232L, 2-shelf, freezer compartment £273   Conforama
Faure   250L, 2-shelf, freezer compartment £311   Conforama
Philips   290L, Combi, fridge-freezer   £436   Conforama
Far   Combi, 210L fridge, 120L freezer   £373   Conforama
Indesit   185L, small freezer compartment   £211   Conforama
Vedette   Combi, 158L fridge, 856L freezer   £372   Cora

Garden Furniture

Holiday homes in the sun need a few pieces of garden or patio furniture, and I would certainly recommend buying these in France. In all the *hypermarchés* mentioned, there are special offers, particularly at the beginning of the season. A few months ago, I bought a monobloc white resin table (six places) and four stacking armchairs for £28. Sun umbrellas vary in price, so if you see a good bargain at home, it is worth buying one there, because you will surely need one. Some random prices include:

Table	170cm x 100cm (8 places), 6 chairs	£71	Montlaur
Table	140cm x 90cm, 4 chairs, parasol, cushions	£56	But
Round table, 4 chairs		£28	But

Earlier this year, before going to France, I bought a sunbed with a good, fat cushion mattress in a local supermarket, at a reduced price of £33. A good buy, I thought. A few weeks later in Carrefour, I found a better one for £21. In Continent, this last summer they were selling off the luxury end of patio loungers, those with an integral drinks tray at arm's length, and delicate white wheels for the butler to transport you to the pool edge, for only £33. Comfortable enough for a spare bed. Replacement mattresses for sun loungers are about £15, on offer. Multiposition relaxer chairs can be bought from about £21. Quality and comfort are excellent. A word of advice: always insist that family and friends put towels on your loungers when sunning themselves. Oil and hot bodies leave indelible stains on fabric. Mine were left in such a mess after one long hot summer that I had to make new loose covers.

DIY

If the average Englishman regards his home as his castle, the average Frenchman, and most of the ones I know, takes enormous pride in actually building his castle. They are avid *bricoleurs* (DIYers). Within moments of entering the house you will be shown *crepi* walls and ceilings, cupboards, staircases, bathrooms tiled from top to toe, workshops containing every possible aid for the keenest *bricoleur*. Incidentally, if you are not yet acquainted with the *crepi* wall finish, you will be.

It is more than likely that any Brit buying a holiday home in France will need to do varying degrees of DIY, and with luck will be pointed in the right direction by neighbours who are as keen for him or her to do the job as correctly as they would themselves.

DIY may well have started out of sheer necessity, but for a large percentage of the population it has become a leisure pursuit, almost a way of weekend life. A *maison* or *apartement secondaire* is not at all uncommon in France. DIY is part of the package, and seems to be quite unrelated to the family's ability to pay a team to do it for them. I knew a Parisian couple living in a chic apartment. She was a leading actress at the *Comédie Française*, he was an art critic on *Le Figaro*. They spent their free time building a holiday home in the Fontainbleau region. And they really were building with their own hands at one point, up to the armpits in bricks and cement, or soaked to the skin sleeping under a leaking roof. Horses for courses, I suppose.

Small wonder that there is a chain of large shops throughout France called Mr Bricolage. Professional builders say they are expensive, but for the amateur, they contain a vast range of house-improving/making artefacts, from bathroom suites to panel pins, from electrical gadgetry to staircases. Frequently there are bargain weeks for bath, loo and bidet sets, which are infinitely cheaper than in the UK. So do not even consider buying in Britain and hiring a van, as I did, to my cost. One loo, when unloaded from the van, had a flush handle missing. Heaven knows what happened to it en route. No amount of searching in Mr Bricolage found a replacement. Well, it just wasn't French, was it? The loo was, ever after, flushable only by the user plunging a hand into the full cistern, and manually lifting the lever. Quite pleasant on a hot day, but chilly in mid-winter.

There is another chain of DIY *hypermarchés*, Bricorama. You could spend a whole day here, and never be bored. This is where you will find bargains and offers galore. Eight years ago, I bought ceramic tiles for my London kitchen floor. At £5 a square metre, they were precisely what I wanted, and a third of the price in the UK. If you are tempted just make sure your car will take the strain. Prices do not seem to have risen very much, either, in this area. For example, last year, from the same *hypermarché*, I bought ceramic tiles for my French kitchen floor, good quality white marble effect, at £6 a square metre.

If you are keen to lay your own ceramic tiles, you will surely find a neighbour with an electric tile cutter. In any case Mr Bricolage shops hire out all kinds of machinery. A steam paper stripper cost me £4 for a weekend.

There was a time when I carted my tool box, with screws, nails, screwdrivers, hammer and power drill, backwards and forwards to France. Inevitably, tools were left behind, or forgotten, and as there was little difference in cost (in fact France has become slightly cheaper) I concluded it was simpler to maintain separate sets. The choice in French DIY aids is much wider, even down to ceramic, brass or wrought-iron door furniture. Three years ago I bought an extending metal ladder in the UK, and took it to France. I need not have bothered. The very same was available, and at the same price.

There is another large chain of DIY stockists, Menuiseries Lapeyre. They are suppliers to the trade, primarily of wood and metal goods, selling doors, window frames, gates, staircases, wrought-iron grilles, balconies, balustrades, and are located throughout France. This is probably where your builder will take you. However, six months ago, I found a better value self-assembly pine staircase, 13 treads and hand rail, in Conforama for £212.

Paint is slightly cheaper in the UK, but the pastel shades available in France are infinite. You will find perfect base colours for 'distressing' that tatty piece of pine into fake *château* 1830. The make 'Valentine' is part of ICI, so you will recognise a few Dulux shades. An eggshell finish is labelled *satinée* and is more popular than gloss.

Wooden curtain poles are cheaper to buy in France than in the UK, as are wooden curtain rings. Incidentally, French curtain rings have no metal eyes attached for the curtain hook, as in the UK. French curtain hooks are made with a built-in attachment which clips on to the rings, doing two jobs for the price of one. Pole brackets are like ours, wood, or, more expensive, brass. Walls are the problem, especially in old houses. We all know the frustration of trying to drill and plug an old crumbling wall when the hole becomes so large as chunks of masonry become dislodged that it has to be filled before it can be plugged.

Obviously sensitive to wall problems, the French have an alternative to fancy brackets, a simple, yet ingenious and cheap article which I have found only in France. It is a slim, but sturdy, steel rod, and comes in two lengths (seven inches and ten inches approximately). At one end is a two-inch perpendicular metal peg, and three inches along is another similar peg. The other end of the rod is fashioned into a sharp point like a spike or skewer. They are sold in pairs and fixing couldn't be easier. You simply hammer the spikes into the wall each side of the window, at the appropriate height for the curtain pole, which will then rest on the rods between the pegs, so it will neither roll off nor fall off. Now the great advantage of these primitive but highly-efficient supports is that you can also attach a pelmet or drapes across the window, from one front peg to the other. Stretch curtain wire hooked on to the pegs works well. I like these steel rods so much that my UK home sports several pairs.

Considering that the French were the main force behind wallpaper manufacture in Europe, and invented the first machine to produce lengths as early as 1739, I have been generally disappointed with what is available between £6 and £12 per roll. All the *bricolage* shops and many *hypermarchés* and furniture stores carry stocks of relatively inexpensive paper, along with specially reduced lines. It is the design in general that I have found disappointing, although occasionally something catches the eye.

Specialist wallpaper and paint shops, as well as fabric and bed linen shops, carry all the sample books, not only for French wallpapers, but also for American brands, plus our own Sanderson, Cole, Colefax and Fowler, G & J Baker and others. On one occasion, thumbing through a pile of books in a rather smart shop, just out of curiosity, as all the papers were £12 – plus-plus-plus, I came across a delightful design. It was a Sanderson, and very popular with the clientele, I was told, because it was so English. However, in this more expensive range, the French score very well.

Designers like Canovas, Nobilis Fontan, Soleiado, Inaltera, Essef, Venilia, etc., produce very high-quality paper and design. All are available in the UK, but obviously there is more choice in the home market, and Essef and Venilia are slightly cheaper.

The most potently 'French' wallpaper for foreign eyes, and perhaps even for the French, must surely be the *toiles*. Venilia make a delightful blue and white at about £16 a roll, and there is a matching fabric. The French led the field in fabric design in the 18th and 19th centuries, and furnishing fabrics in specialist shops continue the tradition. Surprisingly, in the case of most of the beautiful fabrics I openly coveted the price per metre was comfortably modest. Colours are generally strong, with designs, for the most part, traditional. Historically, *toile* design was printed on calico, and lined with *vichy*, the name given to red and white or blue and white two-inch checks. This combination may be a little too powerful for anything less than a *château*-sized room. However, *vichy* on its own is equally attractive and wholly evocative of the *fin de siècle* scene. It can be bought, and very reasonably, too, by the metre, in most open markets.

One last thought. Samples of wallpaper for potential customers, are not, it seems, *de rigueur*. It caused a flutter when I put in a request. It even brought the manager down. I offered to pay, if he could order. Very politely, I was informed that this was not done, but I was most welcome to take the book away, no charge, *naturellement*. All was not lost, though: I wrote to the UK office of the company and was sent enough to paper a door.

Household Goods

When you settle down to holiday home life with a family, the more civilised you become, the more basics turn into essentials. The time comes when besides crockery, cutlery, glasses and saucepans, you will need an iron and ironing board, based on the practical assumption that you will be unlikely to avoid any ironing whatsoever during the hols. Irons are possibly more expensive in France, so it is worth taking one over. Ironing boards, on the other hand, are better value in France. I bought an extra one, and took it back to the UK. Crockery, too, is very good value, provided you look for the special offers, usually 18-piece sets. Apilco and earthenware oven-to-table dishes are excellent buys.

There are also cutlery bargains, certainly in 'bistro' cutlery with coloured handles. For example, in May 1992, I bought in Continent a six-place setting of sturdily-made bistro cutlery, with black and bronze handles, packed into a sealed storage jar, for £11. Admittedly that was a 'special', and I have seen them subsequently for £21, but even that is better than in the UK, where to my horror, I saw the very same package, even the same colour, being advertised as 'Wonderful French Bistro cutlery – superb value at only £32'. At the same time I bought a set of five most attractive butter yellow saucepans with dark blue handles for £17. They were so colourful, and spirit-lifting on a rainy day, I thought the UK would be the best home for them.

Many cleaning products have the same names as ours, but you will find Mir an excellent all-purpose liquid, particularly for ingrained grime. Javel is bleach, good, strong and cheap. Years ago I took over a bucket and mop, but could never find a replacement for the worn mop head, and never remembered to take one over.

In the end, fed up with hands and knees, I bought a French version. It does make sense to buy in France.

Carpets

You may wish to cover your floors with carpets or rugs. There is a carpet shop chain throughout France called Saint-Maclou, which, for me, is a combination of Allied and John Lewis, but better. A 40 per cent wool carpet is about £7-£9 a metre, Polypropyline, £6 or £7. Further up the scale there are some excellent all-wool Berbers. This chain always seems to have special offers or sales. They have a splendid selection of competitively-priced Middle Eastern, Pakistani, Indian and Chinese rugs and carpets.

When my holiday home was in town, I often wondered how my neighbour could grow such a green lawn on such a dry patch of courtyard. It wasn't until I saw her hoovering the patch that the truth dawned. She had bought this remarkably good imitation from Saint-Maclou. At the time I had an eyesore of a flat roof at garden level in the UK. The same commodity at my local DIY was £14.50 a square metre as compared with Saint-Maclou's £9, and for far better quality. I succumbed and brought some home, rolled up in the boot. And there it lies, a plastic piece of France covering my grey flat roof, and to my eyes looking very like the lawn. I make no apologies to purists for this purchase. In fact, I have just put another piece of plastic green down, on an inner courtyard on the terrace of the French house, again from Saint-Maclou, and there has been no increase in price for nearly two years. It was far cheaper to lay a *gazon* than tiling, less onerous than painting stained cement, and it is sympathetic to bare feet.

Carpet indoors is not always the best solution to bad floors in a holiday home, but in warmer regions, so my builder maintains, it is better than vinyl. You generally find, in old houses, that most floors have stone tiles, which says much for the joists supporting them. I loved all the tiles in my present house, the originals, except for the kitchen and a bedroom. Dark red and in poor condition, they always appeared grubby. When the kitchen tiles were replaced, the builder first took up the old ones so as not to add to the weight as we were not at ground level. I bought carpet for the bedroom at £6 a square metre, 50 per cent wool, a special offer from Saint-Maclou. Fitting was to cost £2 a square metre and consequently delivery was free.

The fitter was due at the house, with carpet, at 3.00 p.m. and timing was vital as friends were due to arrive the following morning. As instructed, I had emptied the room of easily movable pieces, including the beds. By 5.00 p.m. there was no sign of the fitter. Several phone calls assured me he was on his way, there had been a delay. By 6.00 p.m. extreme measures had to be taken – after all, the kitchen was piled high with beds and bedding. My voice ringing with Churchillian emotion, I declaredI had never been let down by any other organisation in France, which was true. National pride was touched. The manager, a thin, nervous little man – he works for the council now – assured me, from the bottom of his heart, that despite a collision in which the van had been involved, a close encounter with death, and consequent hospital treatment, the fitter and carpet would get to me somehow. The spirit of Austerlitz was afoot.

At 8.30 they arrived, carpet and fitter. Small and stocky, he worked furiously, perspired copiously, downed several glasses, and assured me that had he a girlfriend at home waiting for him, I would certainly not be seeing him now. I thanked heaven for celibacy.

Meanwhile some doors had to be filed down, and his electric plane had been left in the smashed-up van. No problem. My neighbour Eli was over in an instant with his. By 10.30 p.m. the carpet was down and the doors back in place. French carpet fitters do not leave doors leaning against walls for you to file down and put back, or pay extra. This is part of the carpet layer's job. The doors are usually easier than ours to remove anyway. Instead of large screwed-in hinges, doors – room or cupboard – slot in and lift off.

After an impromptu wine and cheese party, Eli left, leaving me with the carpet fitter. We discussed life, work, ambition, love. He told me about his close friend of 26 who was having a truly beautiful relationship with a woman of 52. He then asked me how old I was. I do not pass on classified information but his guess was generous, so he downed another half bottle. Philosophies homespun and profound continued until midnight, when he took his leave. He said he was really a builder and artist, and gave me his address just in case I should ever need either. The pantechnicon parked in the village square thundered into life. As a parting shot he squeezed out two loud long raspberries on the klaxon, leaving me puzzling over his hospital treatment and injuries, with not a plaster in sight!

When I collected my croissants next morning, everyone, including Henri, knew about my carpet, and at what time the carpet layer left. In fact, had I so wished, the entire village would have made an inspection tour of the floor and, incidentally, got to grips with the carpet layer's pedigree. No prurience this, just straightforward nosiness. It is not for them to pass judgement on how the Englishwoman conducts her private life. *Tant pis*! An attitude I wholeheartedly endorse, and for me, one of the most endearing characteristics of the French.

Washing Machines

Like the telephone, a washing machine was quite out of the question for many years. It was an unaffordable luxury. Not that I was delighted to do mountains of hand washing – on the contrary, much as I loved our French holidays, I frequently had bouts of despair, particularly when beds were changed, to say nothing of towels, beach and bath. When the children were young, we played a game called 'treading the grapes'. I admit it was a terrible cheat, but I felt quite justified. With childish trebles ringing forth, they would stomp and shriek over sheets placed in the shower tray. This worked for a short time, but grubby bare feet often left indelible inscriptions that were difficult to wash off. We gave up that game and returned to an older one called 'Mum will wash them'. Ironically it wasn't until the children were well into doing their own washing that I decided enough was enough, and why should one have more domestic chores on holiday than at home? My automatic Sidex washing machine, bought from the bankrupt shop, was £110. That was nine years ago and it is still working very well, although obviously it is not used consistently throughout the year, a point to consider if you covet that super deluxe machine. A few recent prices:

Rotary	5kg	Automatic	£199	Conforama
Sandra	4kg	Automatic	£173	Conforama
Ariston	5.5kg	Automatic	£223	Conforama
Indesit	5kg	Automatic	£210	Cora
Sidex	5kg	Automatic	£199	But

Television and Radio

Now after nearly 20 years, I have succumbed to an even greater luxury, a television. On the pretext that it would improve my French (not true), and thinking of spending more time at the house in the future, I bought a Pal/Secam 16-inch colour, several stations, for £160, second-hand, of course. It is always better to buy a dual system these days. If the children want to bring their favourite videos from home, you will need a set with a Pal/Secam switch to adapt the system.

If you are interested in buying new, most of the *hypermarchés* have offers fairly regularly, but often they are confined to sets with small screens. If you prefer to rent, the system is similar to that in the UK. Television programmes certainly present an across-the-board impression of a nation's culture. French television has more discussion on an apparently high level. There is a particularly engaging book programme each Friday in which the week's top authors answer questions. The audience is made up largely of young people. There are films, American, and a number of those old French classics. There are far fewer panel games and quiz shows than we are fed in the UK. For the bonus of that alone, it is worth considering emigration. World news coverage is very good. There is even a French journalist reporting regularly from Westminster. So if you keep a dictionary to hand you will be *au fait* with all the doom and gloom. In fact, you will probably know a little more than those at home.

It is worthwhile taking a radio cassette player, even if you cannot leave it behind. French radio has its quota of thumping rock, some indigenous, much imported British and American. However there is a *radio nostalgie*, which, as its name suggests, plays all the old numbers that people of my generation associate with France, from Charles Trenet, Yves Montand, Piaf and Juliette Greco to Jacques Brel, and more. For Radio Three addicts there is *France Musique*, a programme of music and literature. It has its quota of symphonies, *musique concrète*, and some glorious trad jazz. It broadcasts through the night, which is good news for insomniacs. And if French radio should ever have the equivalent of Classic FM, we may well never return to the UK.

Finally a note about the geographical distribution of *hypermarchés*. The same company is likely to trade under several different names, depending on the location, but prices and commodities remain the same. Of course there are several chains bearing a common name throughout France, including Mr Bricolage and Saint-Maclou. Continent can be found in many parts of the country, including stores in Troyes, Caen, Château-Thiery, Quimper, Lille, Beaucaire, St Malo, Reims, Calais, Lyons, Francheville, Chambourcy, Amiens and Sens Orange. There are also branches of Champion in many departements including Aude, Aveyron, Bouches du Rhône, Dordogne, Drome, Ardèche, Gard, Haute Garonne, Herault, Lot, Pyrenées-Atlantiques, Tarn and Var.

If you cannot find any of these *hypermarchés* in your area ask in whichever *hypermarché* is nearest to you whether it belongs to one of these main groups. I should be surprised if the answer were negative.

Chapter Five

The Second-hand Scene

If you are a junk shop fanatic, you will find the second-hand scene in France full of surprises, and very rewarding. If you are not a junk shop fanatic, but need to furnish your house, you will find the second-hand scene equally rewarding. I am a devotee of this worthwhile pastime, often out of necessity, and to prove its worth, there is little of the spanking new in my home. I could happily spend an entire holiday moving from one junk shop to the next without ever being bored, and while I do not expect everyone to share my enthusiasm, the type and quality of furniture to be found in this area is worth noting.

Magasins d'Occasion

In every town there is to be found a *magasin d'occasion*, literally translated, an 'opportunity shop'. Generally, they are full of house clearance furniture, and sometimes soft furnishings. Furniture includes beds, bed heads, bedroom, dining room and sitting room suites, mirrors, armchairs, settees and china. In France, especially in the country areas, house clearance often involves houses in which the old occupants have clung to inherited furniture. So, if you are a traditionalist, you will frequently find in these shops good, well-made, *massif* pieces, old enough to be labelled antique. Of course, there are modern items too, particularly armchairs, settees and rather glitzy sideboards. I bought a *bergère* suite comprising a *canapé* (settee), which doubles as a five-foot bed, and two armchairs for £225. It is not in itself an antique, but the suite is solid oak, and exactly the same design as the original model, somewhere around the turn of the century. In fact, I saw the same suite – a French import – for sale in my local furniture shop at £1245.

French furniture design is on the whole a continuing tradition, which means you still see Louis XIV chairs turned out by the dozen, often unpainted: a gift for distressers. Even the modern ones are *massif.* If you are not a traditionalist, you may not find much to suit your taste beyond a glass-topped table. But there are beds of varying sizes, three-foot, four-foot and the so-called *matrimonial* size, five-foot. You might find a *lit bateau* for between £185 and £250, depending on size, condition and antiquity, or a *lit de traverse*. Again antiques, they were designed for the single sleeper – four-foot wide – and to be pushed into an alcove. Very like the *lit bateau*, the cot side facing the room was decorated and carved, while the wall side was always kept quite plain. I found a walnut *lit de traverse* circa 1850. The wall side was rather in need of veneer repair, but for £150 it was mine. I brought it back to the UK – they dismantle easily – and here it remains, repaired and polished. A good buy, as prices for similar French antique beds in the UK start at about £700. From the same *magasin*, I bought a walnut bed, circa 1910, with exquisite marquetry and ormolu decoration, plus matching *table de nuit*, an elegant, long-legged bedside table with marble top, for £150. After a year they are still shrouded in plastic in my garage, because the room for which they are intended is still awaiting renovation. The inability to resist a bargain, however untimely, and with no immediate usage in mind, is alas, symptomatic of the disease. Not so with my *armoire* however, again from the same shop, which was a piece of furniture I needed. Although *armoires* were originally shelved cupboards, they can be used as wardrobes. They dismantle easily for transport, but a good-sized car boot is essential.

When searching for reasonably-priced furniture, remember that shops bearing the word *brocante* will generally charge you more than the *magasin d'occasion* (see Chapter Six). Each country has its own style and preferences, and decides what is to be savoured and cherished from the past. And *vive la différence*! This is certainly true of the not-so-distant past. For example, many *Henri V* – French Victorian – beds, buffets, tables, *armoires*, jettisoned in vanloads by French grandchildren, are coveted in the UK. My antiquarian chums salivate when they see my pieces of Victorian France. On the other hand, English pine is much sought-after in France, and the prices of imported pieces are sky-high. You will often find in *magasins d'occasion* ensemble sets for sale which the vendor will not split, i.e. bed, commode, king-size wardrobe. The deal is always good value for money, but off-loading unwanted items may be a problem. Six years ago I wanted to buy a large, beautifully carved walnut buffet, but it was being sold with an extending dining table, and six chairs, also walnut, for £450. I was obliged to buy the ensemble. Piece by piece I brought it back to the UK, where I sold the table and chairs, for which I am now truly sorry. The buffet remains my favourite piece of furniture.

Trocs

If you cannot find a *magasin d'occasion* near you, look out for a *troc*, literally a swap or barter shop, and very like its counterpart. Most towns have their *troc*, but there is a chain of larger ones throughout France, the *Troc de l'Isle*. Often I find them more expensive than the smaller shops, but of course the choice is enormous. Here you will find kitchen and bathroom furniture, television sets, electrical goods, rugs, carpets, lighting, and some architectural salvage as well as furniture. The *troc* seems to be a reliable source for television sets: many, including my local, have an arrangement with a well-known French hotel chain. Once a set is two years old, it is sold to the *troc*. All sets are checked out before being put up for sale.

I found kitchen units quite expensive at my local *troc*. In fact, it was cheaper to buy new, probably because the *troc*'s stock were better makes. However, you will find plenty of *frigos* and *congelateurs* (freezers), all reasonably priced. It is always worth investigating before the bankrupt shop. My local *troc* is housed in a large warehouse, and was selling off a large consignment of metal ladders the last time I visited. There are displays of new kitsch, tawdry and over-priced, but if you look carefully you will probably find something of interest.

The best bargains in my experience have been found in the bathroom furniture department. I have bought bidets and washbasins at a fraction of the cost new, and far cheaper than architectural salvage in the UK. Complete with taps, and plunger plugs, bidets are between £7 and £12, and washbasins – you could find one of those broad-rimmed 'Edwardians' – £15 to £25. So before the plumber quotes you for new, look at the *troc*'s stock. And before the builder talks you into buying a new door, check out the *troc*. There is always a large section devoted to doors of every description, plus mantelpieces and surrounds.

Three years ago I bought a three-foot bed, having jettisoned the old camper. It has a beautifully carved oak frame, with tapestry bed heads. It cost £50, and would be classified as an antique in the UK. A six-foot by three-foot ornate gesso frame was another antique I bought at the *troc*. It cost only £18, because it had been painted sludge brown. After stripping it and applying gold leaf polish, I had a mirror cut, and now it has pride of place in my French sitting room. A bargain, certainly, but I was lucky being there the day it came in. Always remember, the turnover in these *trocs* is very fast, and new stock appears daily, so if you cannot find first time, be patient, and try again.

Markets

France, as any Francophile knows, abounds with magnificent markets, and not just for foodstuffs. The market is where you will find cloth by the metre: provençal cotton, plains, checks (£3.50 to £4.30 per metre); heavy velours (£8.75 to £10 per metre); Italian brocades and plenty of special offers. If there is any particular curtaining or loose cover fabric you need for the UK home, bring the measurements with you on your next visit. Once I hazarded a very wrong guess, so now I come prepared.

Last year on a household linen stall, I bought a piece of double duvet-size cotton for £11. It was a type of Madras check, and a good heavy weave. It made up into four cushion covers, a tablecloth, and curtains for my UK kitchen. On market stalls you will find good quality cotton sheets, fitted and flat, for £4 to £7.50 for a single. *Hypermarchés* also sell cotton sheets, singly, for just a little more. *Couettes* (duvets) can be found in both. Big continental pillows are not as easy to find these days. A few years ago, all the *hypermarchés* and markets sold them, but now you have to search a little. The new ones are smaller squares than their forebears. Why should they abandon tradition? Perhaps it's the effect the EEC. Heaven forbid French pillows should be further reduced to our oblongs!

Friperies

There is one place, however, where you *will* find the good, old-fashioned, down mega-pillow – the *friperie*. These '*frips*' are countrywide centres for second-hand clothing, bedding, and bed linen. Our local *frip* looks like Stalag 15 from the outside, and not much different inside. It's the contents that matter. If you can imagine Oxfam, a smart designer dress agency and a Bath antique linen shop all under one roof, that's a *frip*. The goods for sale are a complete *mêlée*, and are far from well-presented, but all articles are spotlessly clean, and it is up to you to search. I have bought linen sheets with embroidered initials, exquisitely lace-edged, for between £7.50 and £12. Plain linen or cotton, perhaps with initials, cost about £7.50. For me, the fact they are second-hand adds to their value, and they are always whiter than white. Mega-pillowcases are the great finds here. Some have never been used, and dusty brown fold marks from years in a dowry drawer are plain to see. Initials are elaborately embroidered on some, and lace frilling decorating the edges is often hand-made and quite beautiful. They cost between £3.75 and £7.50, and you could buy similar – French imports – in Bath and Chelsea for £17 to £25. I have now accumulated about two dozen, and frankly I cannot stop. They make excellent presents, too.

In the *frip*, you will find down mega-pillows for £5 to £6. They are clean, but I always have mine dry cleaned – cheaper in France than in the UK, incidentally. I buy all my duvet covers –

housses de couette – at the *frip*, very good heavy cotton weave, for £7.50, generous single size. No fancy colours or patterns, plain white, but so much better than bobbly polycotton. Cotton lace is more difficult to find in the *frip*, but you will find some mixtures, and yards of nylon or terylene curtaining, heavier curtains, and bedspreads.

Now a word about clothes. Much of the *frip*'s stock comes from Germany and Switzerland, and designer labels are not uncommon. Perhaps not quite last year's fashion, but if you like it and it fits, you will not have spent a fortune. And men are catered for, too, in this department.

A well-known actor friend bought a loden overcoat, hardly, if ever, worn, pockets still stitched, with caped shoulders, and in traditional dark green, for £37. Some garments are straight from a bankrupt factory, or even an old catwalk. I bought a heavy cream silk trouser suit, perfect fit, factory fresh, unworn, and labelled Pierre Cardin, for £12. Now my daughters tell me that Pierre Cardin sold his label, and that the trousers are very very *passé*. Who cares? The jacket alone is excellent, and the trousers could well make a surprise comeback. There is no stigma attached to being seen at the *frip*, everyone goes there, locals, local British, and visitors.

Not all visitors wish to be seen there, however. I was invited to a dinner party given by some local English friends. Among the guests was a London barrister's wife. During the course of dinner she made several disparaging remarks about the country, and the usual 'colonial' comments on plumbing and quaint workmen. Dangerous stuff, as we were all fairly devoted Francophiles. Her other remarks confirmed that one could be truly civilised only by living in London, and be happy only by living in the heart of

Mayfair, presumably surrounded by one's staff. The next day I was rummaging through blouses and skirts at the *frip* when to my surprise I saw herself of the previous evening rummaging through the same rail. She spotted me, but pointedly avoided eye contact. I waited until she was at the cash desk paying for her second-hand before engaging her in a very one-sided conversation. The woman was acutely embarrassed. I hope she enjoyed wearing her French second-hand – in W1, of course!

If you have no *frip* nearby, there is always a *frip* stall on market day. In our market we have several long trestle tables of sheets, lace (mixture) curtains, pillowcases, tablecloths, bib aprons, lace handkerchiefs, drawer sheets, bolster cases and duvet covers. Another trestle carries jumpers, coats, jeans, rather like the village jumble sale, and you are not likely to find any designer gems. However, even here I have picked up good-quality silk scarves for a few francs. There are rails and rails of white cotton blouses, nightshirts, nightdresses, camisoles, chemises: in fact a complete Laura Ashley wardrobe circa 1920.

I remember my eldest daughter, at 14, decked out in flowing white nightdresses from morning till night. The wearing of a big floppy hat signified that she was dressed for the day, and in full command of her senses. Well, more or less – she was in love at the time, and what could be more romantic than a stroll through a lavender field, dressed for a latter-day Monet? The *frip* stall has much to answer for.

Emmäus

Emmäus is a charitable organisation, contributed to by the Red Cross and other charities, devoted to the sale of the second-hand.

Every so often sales are held of household goods and furniture. Emmäus, like the others, is a nationwide organisation. Although the sales are advertised, they are easily missed, but your nearest tourist information centre or Mairie will tell you.

In conclusion, the second-hand scrummage becomes, in time, an affliction. There is no cure. Start if you dare.

Chapter Six

Upmarket Furniture

Brocante and Antiques

Brocante means junk or second-hand, but generally today's *brocanteurs* see themselves on the antique periphery, and their prices reflect that belief. *Brocante* and *antiquités* are usually coupled together for *foires* (fairs) and markets. *Brocante* shops frequently carry interesting stock, even verging on the antique, but personally, I have yet to find a reasonable purchase in any one of them. That is not to say that you won't. Antique shops make no concessions to bargain-hunters. They sell the best, and they expect the best prices. As in the UK, furniture is very well-presented, polished and cared for. Stepping inside is akin to entering a cathedral, where the minimum of body movement is expected, along with reverential vocal tones: precisely how the custodians of such treasures expect anyone who is 'just looking' to behave. They know a *sans culotte* when they see one. For the real purchaser, the one with monetary intent, Madame, who has instinctively sniffed him out from the start, will cast her knitting aside, rise gracefully out of the Louis *chaise*, and smile. For us, the peasants, there are sights of irritation, and monosyllabic responses to questions. That is why I rarely visit smart antique shops in France. It is like going to a Bond Street counterpart in scruffy clothes carrying a plastic bag from C&A.

In my experience the best *brocante* is to be found in the open markets, where you can do some haggling and, depending on the time of day, and what sort of day they have had, can often do very well. If you visit one of these markets, go prepared to be tempted. Take cash, or your French chequebook. Credit cards, travellers' cheques and Eurocheques are not welcome, particularly the latter, as the dealer has to pay the bank a handling percentage.

The first *brocante/antiquités* fair I visited some 15 years ago was like an Aladdin's cave (perhaps not exactly cave, as it was in the open air). It was held in a small market town. Somewhere in the middle was an enormous open space, almost as big as the town itself, filled with rows upon rows of stands and dealers. There were exquisite pieces, magnificent mirrors of Napoleonic provenance, *lits bateaux* by the dozen, and enormous *armoires*. There were delicate Louis XV painted bureaux, commodes, chairs, *chaises*, armchairs, and rows of *pries Dieu* going for a song. There were lengths of old lace, brocade curtains, cushions, bed covers, and even elaborate wrought-iron gates, which must have graced a *château*. I fell for a mirror, circa 1850. The top half was a Watteauesque painting, and the frame, gesso and gold leaf, was in near perfect condition. The dealer agreed to £35. Even then it was a bargain. I had no cash with me, only an English chequebook, but I had money at home, and gave him instructions to find and deliver. I have never seen him from that day to this.

I make a point of visiting this fair every year, making sure now that I have cash and my French chequebook, should temptation rear its head. Nothing has changed except the prices and my interest. Both have risen. Last year on my annual pilgrimage I noticed a stand run by a couple of heavily-bearded Spaniards, displaying antique metalware. There was a pair of ornate five-branched bronze and brass candelabra, with snuffers. During the course of the day I returned to gaze, several times. Eventually, I bought the pair for £55. Later, when I examined them carefully, and saw familiar Latin inscriptions around the bases, the truth dawned. They had surely fallen off a Spanish church. No wonder the dealers had been keen to get rid of them.

Fairs are fun, even if you are not interested in buying. Here you can be a *sans culotte* with the rest, just come for the *frites* and *saucisses* on sale at the various booths scattered throughout. The children will love it, provided you can manacle busy fingers when skirting close to priceless porcelain. Or you can sit more elegantly, drinking wine and overlooking the *mêlée*. Naturally, these fairs are full of foreign dealers, and the British are always well represented. The expense of the journey has to be covered by the mark-up on the furniture bought, to say nothing of dealer profit. I often wonder how many times pieces change hands before they reach their optimum in an antiquarian's *salon*.

Two years ago at a fair I bought a marble *table de toilette*, pure and attractive French Victoriana, and compared with British prices it was very reasonable. Last year I found a turn-of-the-century marble café table on a wrought-iron base. The dealer, a jovial Breton, started off at £90. I waited until the end of the day, and bought it for £60.

Early French lace – from about the late 18th century – can still be found, and as manual traditions of lace-making seem to have continued, particularly in rural areas, you are likely to find hand-made panels at these fairs. They are not cheap, but beautiful, and you will certainly have a one-off. Recently I bought an eight-metre by two-metre cream cotton lace curtain, with hand-crocheted panels, for £75.

There is an open air *brocante* market each Monday at my nearest large town. Here some years ago I bought an early 18th-century brass bed corona, ornate, unusual, and one of a pair. It was the end of the day, and I was offered the pair for £50. At the time I could not afford both.

At the same market I bought a rococco design gold leaf pelmet for £20. The bird on the central pinnacle has lost its wings now, but one day I shall attempt a repair. Pelmets and coronas are obviously not popular in my neck of the French woods, for which I am grateful.

These weekly markets are where you will find the good decorative artefacts for your home, especially mirrors, frames and prints. The best time to buy is in the autumn and winter – I find summer prices far too geared to the tourist trade. Once you have a house, you will cease to feel like a tourist. In fact, you will begin to regard them with the same benign amusement as the locals. Over the years, having brought back so many articles, large and small, to my UK home, I never feel completely out of touch with my place in the sun, even on the dreariest winter morning.

Some years ago, the children and I spent a night at Barbizon, near Fontainebleau. We visited the hostelry where the painters of the Barbizon school and their literary friends, Georges Sand and Alfred de Musset, stayed when the plague hit Paris. Two years later I was scavenging in a Paddington junk shop – and it really was junk – when, to my everlasting surprise, I found, in a tatty frame, an original etching, signed and dated, of Barbizon's one and only main street, showing the hostelry, and our hotel on the opposite side of the road. I bought it for pennies. The date is '51'. Judging by the cobblestones and tumbledown façades, I thought it had to be 1851. Then a friend pointed out the delicately-pencilled shape of a motorbike reposing under a tree. You can't win them all!

If, like me, you are interested in antiques and *brocante*, there is nothing more infuriating than finding you have just missed the annual bun fight, or even the weekly jamboree, which everybody knows about except you. I have therefore compiled the following lists, which may help avoid frustration. All the markets listed are made up of professional vendors and dealers who are known and registered, in case of any problem. Some markets have fly-by-night amateurs, little better than car-boot salesmen, and you will never see them again.

There are literally dozens of yearly and twice-yearly antique/ *brocante* fairs throughout France. Some specialise, for example, in old books, prints, paintings, *objets* from the 18th century, *toiles* and old fabric. Those listed are vendors of general antique/*brocante* and have been selected simply because they seem to cover the length and breadth of France. Precise dates cannot be given as they vary from year to year, but all you have to do, if you are interested, is contact the local Mairie.

Yearly and Twice-Yearly Markets

JULY
    Amboise (Ile d'Or)
    Meze (near Montpellier and Sete)

JULY-AUGUST
   Avranches (Mont Saint-Michel)
   Béziers

AUGUST
   Barjac
   Cannes
   Evian (Swiss frontier)
   L'Isle sur La Sorgue
   Orange (Palais de la Foire)
   Pont l'Eveque (Calvados)
   Port de Lanne
   Valbonne

SEPTEMBER
   Avignon (Parc des Expositions, Autoroute A7 exit
      Avignon Sud)
   Cagnes sur Mer (between Nice and Antibes)
   Chartres (Parc des Expositions)
   Clermont-Ferrand
   Issoudun
   Lac d'Aiguille (Autoroute A7 exit Valence Nord)
   Le Havre (Palais des Expositions)
   Paris (Parc Floral Bois de Vincennes)

OCTOBER
   Paimpol (Chateau de Kersa Ploubazlanec)
   Villefranche en Beaujolais

NOVEMBER
   Paris (Espace Wagram)

Do remember, this list is only the tip of the iceberg. Wherever you are in France you will certainly find a *foire* right through the year.

   In addition to these mega-markets, there are monthly and weekly antique/*brocante* markets in almost every sizeable town. Sometimes they coincide with the regular market, as in Nîmes, for example, so if one of you is a junk fan, at least the other can buy the veg. Just to the south-east of Avignon is L'Isle sur la Sorgue, a delightful town almost entirely devoted to antiques and *brocante*. Quite apart from the annual *grande foire*, some dealers are operating here every day of the week, and more at weekends. The place is full of inviting cafés and restaurants, and there is a particularly attractive 'English' tea room adjoining the large warehouse, which houses a hundred or so dealers over its three floors.

Selected List of Monthly Antique/*Brocante* Markets

SATURDAYS

Bagnols Sur Ceze	3rd Sat
Béziers	1st Sat
Bordeaux	1st Sat
Bourg-en-Bresse (Square Lalande)	3rd Sat
Chambery	2nd Sat
Cherbourg (Place des Moulins)	1st Sat
Clermont-Ferrand (Place du ler Mai)	1st Sat
Evreau (Halle des Expositions)	1st Sat
Givors	3rd Sat
Nancy (Vielle Ville)	2nd Sat
Riom	2nd Sat
Stes Maries de la Mer	1st and 3rd Sat
Valence (Parc Expositions)	2nd and 4th Sat

SUNDAYS

Amiens (Place Parmentier)	2nd Sun
Bergerac (Vieux)	1st Sun
Blois (Place Ave Maria)	2nd Sun
Cahors (Place Rousseau)	4th Sun
Cannes (La Bocca)	1st Sun
Chartres (Place St Pierre)	4th Sun
Dijon (Ancienne Patinoire)	Last Sun
Fréjus	4th Sun
Hyères (Marché aux Fleurs)	1st Sun
La Ciotat	3rd Sun
Le Mans	2nd Sun
Limoges:	2nd Sun
Marseilles (Cours Julien)	2nd Sun
Milly la Forêt	2nd Sun
Montelimar (Rue Ste Croix)	2nd Sun
Moulins	2nd Sun
Nevers (Place Mosse)	3rd Sun
Poitiers	4th Sun
Salon de Provence (Parc Expositions)	1st Sun
Reims (Zone Industrielle)	1st Sun
Toulouse	1st Sun
Troyes	3rd Sun

MONDAYS

Chartres (Place St Pierre)	4th Mon
Grenoble (Place St André)	3rd Mon

OTHER

Toulouse	1st Fri

Weekly Markets

SATURDAYS
  Aix-en-Provence
  Albi
  Angers
  Arles
  Bordeaux
  Limoges
  L'Isle sur la Sorgue
  Monaco
  Nantes
  Orléans
  Paris (Porte de Montreuil)
  Paris (St Ouen)
  Paris (Square G. Brassens)
  Rouen
  Tours

SUNDAYS
  Alès
  Clermont-Ferrand
  Hyères (Av de la Pinede)
  Lille
  Limoges
  L'Isle sur la Sorgue
  Montpellier (Espace Mosson)
  Paris (Porte de Montreuil)
  Paris (St Ouen)
  Paris (Square G. Brassens)

SUNDAYS (continued)
  Perpignan
  Rouen
  St Etienne
  Toulon (Parc Expositions)

MONDAYS
  Limoges
  L'Isle sur la Sorgue
  Nice
  Nîmes
  Paris (Porte de Montreuil)
  Paris (St Ouen)

TUESDAYS
  Aix-en-Provence

WEDNESDAYS
  Tours

THURSDAYS
  Aix-en-Provence
  Rennes

FRIDAYS
  Grenoble
  Poitiers

Chapter Seven

To Let or Not to Let

The advantage of letting your *bijou* place in the sun is threefold. Revenue received will enable you to:

1. Pay for running costs.
2. Put aside towards future improvements.
3. Pay for your holiday.

The disadvantages can be multifold. It all depends on the tenants. Even if you know them or their kinfolk, it is no guarantee that all will be well. Frequently the reverse applies. Complete strangers can show more care for your house and contents, and are more likely to replace breakages. A small point, but worth noting: don't ever let to tenants who have no other home – you could be in trouble. If you do wish to consider a long let at some stage you would be well advised to go through an agency so that you are legally protected.

To let successfully is dependent upon the individuals on both sides. The keynote is honesty. In the first instance, the landlord should never mislead any prospective tenant by 'talking up' a cottage into a *manoir*. If rooms are unfurnished or incomplete, say so, and if it is an hour from the nearest watering-hole, say that, too. Equally, state if it has balconies dangerous for small children.

On the subject of small children, some friends, well-versed in the letting business, gave me sound advice: never let to families with under-fives, unless you know and trust them or the children are young enough for carrycots. That may sound a little harsh, but one year I lost two mattresses, despite having been promised that the offspring were dry, and that in any case they would have rubber sheets just in case. Neither was true. The mattresses had to be thrown away, and I had no redress.

What to Provide

Before you consider letting, think about what you should provide. Kitchen utensils, tea towels, crockery, cutlery, saucepans, iron and ironing board are essentials, a washing machine is not. If you are not providing bed linen, this limits your prospective tenants to car travellers. Sheets for a family of four take up far too much suitcase space. Towels, however, are not usually provided. Be prepared to buy, and keep in stock, washing-up liquid, household cleaning materials, kitchen towels, loo paper and light bulbs. People staying for a week or two will not feel inclined to buy these goods, and neither should they, in my opinion.

Sun chairs and patio tables are also essential for 'sun' holidays, but make it a rule that all fabric loungers are covered by the sun worshipper's towel. This will not always be adhered to, as you will find out, and of course it is impossible to point the finger. I was obliged to renew one or two lounger cushions every year, and found a cigarette burn on the patio table, which had to be considered a calculated loss.

Before letting, empty wardrobes, and however many drawers you deem necessary, of personal belongings. If you do not have a lock-up storage cupboard, storing your belongings in plastic bags on top of the wardrobe works just as well. Remove and store any precious *objets*.

The commodity most susceptible to wear and tear in a season of lets is glass. Balloon glasses, nothing fancy, are aesthetically pleasing and cheap to buy and replace. No matter what agreement tenants have signed, replacing broken glasses is rarely on their agenda, unless they happen to be particularly conscientious. This casual attitude often applies to other artefacts. I had a pair of matching bedside lamps. Friends of friends stayed, and after their departure one lamp was found to be broken. Nothing was said, no recompense offered, although they were given the opportunity. Had they been strangers, I should have asked. Another matching pair of lamps had to be bought, and the episode written off to experience.

I have a kitchen cupboard full of condiments, herbs, tea, coffee, and assorted tinned stuff – emergency stock. I tell everyone who stays at the house that they may use the condiments and emergency stock, particularly on arrival, but if they use it consistently, the commodity should be replaced. This has never been abused.

For short stays there is little point in monitoring gas and electricity: it is better to include it in the rental. If you have bottled gas for cooking, keep a spare standing by. If the spare has been used up and the tenants have to pay for a refill, reimburse them on their return to the UK.

Many years ago, an MP and his wife took my house for a week. They were clearly unused to gas bottles and refills, for upon their return I was sent a hefty bill, not just for a refill, but for a new bottle, plus a new contract with a different supplier. The fact that my information sheet told them precisely where to buy refills if needed, and the cost, and that no one before or since has ever made such an error, confirms my general opinion of the House of Commons and those who govern.

Housekeepers

To let successfully, it is important to have a good back-up system organised in your absence. Things are less likely to go badly wrong with a good *femme de ménage*. This is easier said than done, I know. Good housekeepers, like a good workforce, take time to locate. Recommendation is one way, and someone living nearby, known to neighbours, is another. The average you should expect to pay is £4.50 to £5 per hour. The minimum rate in France is now £4.50 per hour.

I have interviewed several ladies over the years, and have made mistakes. The genial, jovial personality does not necessarily signify a conscientious attitude towards your house and its wellbeing. Be wary of employing someone who already has a fairly full work schedule, and her own domestic responsibilities. No matter how much she may appear to want to keep your house and its guests in order, you will be offering only seasonal work, and there are no prizes for guessing whose house will be short-changed in a busy week. Unless there is a personal recommendation, always ask for references. A housekeeper for an absentee owner will be expected to wash and iron bed linen, make up beds, keep cupboards tidy and clean the house ready for incoming guests. And all this in your absence, and to your specific agenda. Incidentally, I have always drawn up a specific work agenda for my housekeepers, and carefully gone through it, point by point. Usually, it has been a complete waste of time and effort. Only one has ever assiduously followed a work schedule, my present one, and she is by far the best. It is important to try out your housekeeper while you are *in situ*. You will need someone with initiative and a responsible attitude towards her work. If she is called *serieuse* by the neighbours, you have probably chosen well. In addition to house cleaning, she will be responsible for turning the services on and off, and for replenishing the stock of household commodities. It is always worth paying a good housekeeper for a little more time than you estimate. In the holiday period, there may be a quick turnabout, with guests leaving and arriving on the same day. In order to help the housekeeper, make sure that outgoing guests leave by midday, and that incoming ones do not arrive before four o'clock.

I have made the wrong choice more than once in the past, and it is inevitable that difficulties arise when the prospect of disengagement looms, for a loose type of friendship will have developed between you and the housekeeper. But, and here's the rub, unless you are a fly on the wall you will never know the standard of her efficiency in your absence, except when tenants complain. About four years ago I had a wonderful, laughing, jolly helper. We were on first-name terms, and shared many laughs, as well as family confidences. She was a workaholic, and fitted me in with her several jobs. She made more than a meagre living, as she ran her own car, and took holidays abroad, as well as appearing to support an invalid husband, who was as dull as she was jolly. While she would work like a Trojan in my presence, in my absence the situation was rather different, as it transpired. Breathlessly charging from A to B, and with no supervision, she severely short-changed my establishment. The beds were changed and clean, but frequently the *frigo* was left untouched, with bits of festering food inside. I should never have known had not two old friends had the good sense to tell me. On this occasion, for her five hours work, only the beds – two – had been changed, so my guests set to, and cleaned up the house. I telephoned others who had stayed, and they all confirmed lapses of one sort or another. My jolly madame was far from pulling her weight. It was difficult to sack her, as I liked her, so I tried to drop hints about my very pernickety friends who were coming to stay, and how they would complain to me if all were not perfect.

All this was done with smiles and eyebrows shrugging up and down, whereupon she threw up her hands and laughed until the tears rolled down her red cheeks. She had never heard of friends like that, and in any case I shouldn't worry, after all she was there. She would tell them to go and sit in the sun if they didn't like the house. So, *tant pis*! Not the result I had hoped for. To avoid further problems I added a paragraph to the agreement form.

Eventually I was able to avoid a confrontation only because I moved, and the new house was undergoing renovation and repairs for nearly three years. For much of that period it was only fit for family. Meanwhile, she found herself a full-time job, and when the time was right, I found an excellent young woman in the village, who is *très serieuse*. Jolly Madame and I are still friends.

One of the great advantages of having domestic back-up, quite irrespective of guests or tenants, is knowing that when you arrive the shutters will be open, electricity and water turned on, the house cleared of cobwebs, and the beds made up. When you leave, you know that the bins will be emptied, the *frigo* defrosted, sheets washed and put away and shutters closed until next time. For 15 years I packed in a frenzy of cleaning, checking and double-checking, and when I finally sat at the steering wheel I was almost too tired to drive.

Agreements and Information

An agreement form should be sent to everyone who borrows or rents your house, be they friends or strangers. If you are in any doubt as to the outline format, here is a typical example. Add or subtract according to your own particular needs:

HOLIDAY LET AGREEMENT

BETWEEN

     LANDLORD ....

AND

     TENANT ....

Whereby the latter agrees to rent a furnished house, namely,

ADDRESS ....

....

From ....(date of arrival)

To   ....(date of departure)

At   .... per week, payable in ....

THE TENANT AGREES:

1. To remain at..........(ADDRESS)...........for the appointed time only, unless otherwise arranged with landlord.
2. To leave by midday on the final day, and to arrive no earlier than four o'clock, to give the housekeeper time to prepare the house.

3. To replace or renew any items broken or damaged during the holiday.

While every effort is made to maintain a high standard of cleanliness in the house, the landlord would welcome any helpful suggestions. These should be made directly to the housekeeper.

THE LANDLORD AGREES TO PROVIDE:

Electricity
Gas
Hot water
Bed linen
House linen (except towels)
Cleaning services before arrival and after departure

If agreed, please return this form, signed, together with a deposit of ....% of total rental.
Remaining ....% to be paid not less than six weeks before departure. House keys will then be forwarded, to be returned as soon as is convenient after the holiday.

Signed ....Tenant
....Address

Signed ....Landlord
....Address

Included with the tenancy form should be information sheets, covering the following points:

1. The house: details of accommodation – beds – washbasins – bathrooms – sizes of communal rooms – seating around dining or kitchen table – floors – carpets/tiles – cooking equipment – freezer – washing machine etc.
2. The environs: the village or town – walks – local places of interest – public transport and car hire.
3. Shops, restaurants and bars: give a price range if possible.
4. Places of interest a drive away: historical monuments – parks – nature reserves – archaeological sites.
5. Activities: swimming – canoeing – horse-riding – surfing – scuba diving.
6. Local and easily reachable events: fêtes – festivals – markets.

Obviously, photographs are important. There is no need to send originals – you may not see them again. In any case photocopying is usually perfectly adequate. It is wise and businesslike to take a deposit on booking, which is refundable only up to six weeks before the start of the holiday; even with friends, and even if they are taking your house at break-even rates.

However well you know your tenants, always be businesslike about letting, and be aware of any extra words that may be added by the tenant to your agreement form. You may think, as I did, that a simple 'from...to...' will specify the dates of arrival and of departure. But if a prospective tenant adds the word 'inclusive', beware.

It never occurred to me that 'inclusive' could mean the next day – far more complicated than a simple 'from...to...'. Thinking no more about it, I had prearranged with my housekeeper that she should clean the house on the Friday after midday, when the holidaying family friends would have left, and prepare for the incoming doctor's family, due to arrive at six. I received a telephone call from the doctor's wife at precisely six o'clock. They were at the house, which was apparently occupied but resembled the *Marie Celeste*. There was no sign of the previous occupants, and certainly no sign of packing. Being so far away I was fairly frantic, and to add to the problem my housekeeper was not at home. The new family set to, emptied wardrobes and drawers, and tried to settle in. Meanwhile the 'inclusive' family returned, and there were more telephone calls. Fortunately they took it reasonably – they were friends – and I paid for a night's accommodation in a nearby hotel – for five of them. Had they been difficult, a lawyer friend assures me that the law would have been on my side. The wording on an agreement form should *not* be altered, or added to. Now I always include 'date of arrival' and 'date of departure', to avoid confusion.

Finding Tenants

You may decide to advertise for tenants. *The Lady* magazine seems to be a favourite with British friends resident in France, and by comparison its advertising rates are very reasonable. The quality Sunday papers are another advertising area, but far more expensive. Most families want to take holidays in August, and as that is when you'll probably be wanting the house, the letting period is limited. It is therefore not worth spending too much on advertising for only a three- or four-month availability. I would suggest a trial run in January or February, in one publication.

You may well have sufficient response just from that. Most of the quality papers try to sell special offers of two or three consecutive weeks. A good idea for a hotel or a complex, maybe, but for one holiday home, it is not worth the expense, in my opinion. If you place an advertisement, don't forget to have several copies of your agreement forms and information sheets standing by. One should always live in hope!

As French estate agents are feeling the cold as much as our own, many are taking on *maisons secondaires* for house lettings. This is probably the most painless method for any householder. The agent will take a photograph of your house and sign a rental agreement including a pro rata percentage for him. For your part, you are asked to fill in a detailed inventory of everything, down to the teaspoons. Upon termination of the tenancy, the agent checks through the list before the tenants actually leave. As the letting agent's catchment area includes advertising in France, Holland, Germany, Switzerland and Belgium, the odds are in your favour. If you have central heating, these agencies often specialise in long winter lets. This is advantageous as it keeps the house aired and repaired.

In time you will not have to look for tenants. Word spreads between family and friends, and friends of friends.

Rents

Rents vary like the length of the proverbial piece of string. On average, for a house with reasonable facilities, sleeping six, with one or two bathrooms (or one bathroom and washbasins), washing machine and/or dishwasher, bed linen, cleaning before and after, you could expect £300 to £350 per week in high season. Generally, this means the last two weeks of July, the whole of August, and the first two weeks of September.

Mid-season is usually June, July, September and October, and you could expect £250 to £300 per week.

Low season is a matter of choice, and depends to a large extent on location. For anywhere south of Lyons, in May and June you could expect £200 to £250. For long winter lets it is far better to ask a very modest rent, say £75 to £100, and to have the tenants pay for all services.

These figures are average, and are taken from a cross-section of friends who let their properties. Where you are will determine what you ask. If you have a villa with a swimming pool, you will command a higher rent. If you have a villa with a swimming pool outside Cannes, you will receive an even higher rent.

On second thoughts, if you have a villa with pool outside Cannes, what are you doing reading a budget book?

Chapter Eight

You and Your Bank

Bills for keeping your house warm, watered and fed, arrive either half-yearly or every two months, in the case of France Telecom. Non-payment, or even late payment, usually results in the guillotine. A bank account is therefore a must. If you have bought your house with a mortgage you will already have one, but if your only bank is in the UK, think again. There are, in France, as in Britain, big high street banks, such as Credit Lyonnais and Credit Agricole, which are more likely to be found in out-of-the-way provincial towns than smaller banking establishments. The Caisse d'Epargne, a slightly different type of bank, is also to be found everywhere. This is essentially a savings bank – a cross between the Post Office and a building society. They take cash deposits from nationals and foreigners alike, and they also have a mortgage service for house purchase.

Overdrawing and Account Management

Banking in France is to be taken very seriously. In the UK we may joke about our overdrafts. In France it is no joke. I used to wonder why shopkeepers rarely asked for identification when presented with a cheque. The answer is simple: it is a criminal offence to be overdrawn. Our banks have a habit of sending unpleasant letters; French banks go one step further. They give you 15 days to replenish diminished funds. If no money is forthcoming they freeze your account and withold your chequebook – for a year!

This happened to me six years ago. I was holidaying in Bulgaria, and for various reasons I was not able to return at the appointed time. During the course of this delay I was unable to pay any money into my French account, and a few cheques had been drawn on it. Nevertheless, I thought I had enough in the account to break even. On returning to the UK, I received a letter informing me that my account was to be frozen for a year, and demanding that I return my chequebook forthwith. The frozen account had already been reported to the holy of holies, the Banque de France, and any attempt on my part to open an account at any other bank would result in criminal charges being brought by the police. I talked at length to my bank manager who, although sympathetic, could do nothing as the decision had been taken by head office. At this stage, even replenishing the account by the fastest possible means would have had no effect whatsoever. It was a *fait accompli*. And all because I was overdrawn by £30!

When such decisions can be taken with little, or in my case, no notification it is vital to know exactly, at any given moment, what you have in your account. Although my French bank, unlike my English bank, sends statements with reasonable regularity, certain services, such as EDF/GDF, frequently hold your cheque for weeks before paying it in. In the meantime, you could be blissfully ignorant of the real state of affairs. For this reason I will not be seduced by persistent pleas from all the services to pay bills by *prélèvement* (standing order). What's the French for 'once bitten'? Of course, this situation only applies if you, like me, live a hand-to-mouth existence.

This experience taught me to be aware of French bank statements, and their close relationship with cheque stubs. At the start of every holiday I now call on the bank manager and go through my account to make sure all cheques written have been presented.

When we bought our first *ruine* and work was started, I kept the accounts because no one else would. We knew vaguely what was being paid in, and exactly what was being paid out. This went on uneventfully for two years. In retrospect I see that these were indeed the halcyon days of the relationship between the bank and me, the days of naïve trust, when every bank was infallible, and every bank manager a mini pope. Imagine my surprise, therefore, at receiving a letter summoning me to an audience with the manager, without delay. Trembling, I was ushered into the papal suite and offered a cup of coffee. Was this the prisoner's last meal, I wondered? The manager then told me that a certain sum of money had been wrongly credited to my account. Another Briton, with a name looking like mine, at least to French eyes, had deposited cheques in a Paris bank, and they had subsequently winged their way into my account, light years away in the sticks. The bank would therefore expect me to pay back the money, though not all at once, *naturellement*. I was aghast, but the pope smiled.

For the next few days I lived in a mound of bank statements, and they seemed to square up with what I had paid in. Frankly, I could not see where the mistake had been made. However, they insisted, and continued to insist. Of course we had paid in numerous cheques, but because I had mislaid the paying-in slips there was no way of detailing them. After a year I had paid back a very small amount of this so-called debt. But the salad days were over, and my confidence in this well-known bank was non-existent.

There was nothing to be done except withdraw my funds. I went to another bank, where I have lived happily ever after. As far as I was concerned, the mythical debt could remain. As the bank has never contacted me from that day, 15 years ago, to this, I can only assume that on closer scrutiny, it transpired that the error may never have occurred. After all, it is unusual for a bank not to pursue a debt. On the other hand, if they owe you, mum appears to be the word.

Cautionary tales like these appear to confirm the absolute power of the French bank. But there is one civic official who seems to have even greater power, the Commune's *percepteur*, to be found at the Bureau de Perception (see Chapter One). I was unaware of the power vested in him until a few months ago when, out of the blue, I received a letter from my bank's legal department deeply regretting to inform me that the *percepteur* of the town where I used to live had just sent them an *avis à tiers detenteur* for the sum of 3866F. In other words, until this sum had been paid to the *percepteur*, my bank account would be blocked. The Bureau de Perception kindly gave me three weeks to settle the account. The bank was powerless.

I had absolutely no idea why I could possibly owe such a sum and for what, as I had moved from the town, and the clutches of that particular *percepteur*, in May 1989. Frankly, I could not face another year of blocked account, so several frantic telephone calls ensued. The mystery was finally solved. My bank's legal department were extremely courteous and helpful throughout, making several telephone calls on my behalf. According to the Bureau, I owed water rates, *taxes foncière* and *taxes d'habitation* for the best part of 1988 and 1989. Baffling indeed, as I had already had an altercation over water rates just before moving out of town.

It transpired that the Bureau had lost my current UK address, so had raked up an old one which I had left in 1986. So, for four years, demands galore must have been sent to this address, and to no avail. Surely, I asked, if they knew my bank, the Bureau could have discovered my correct address? Simple enough, but they had no answer to that. I collected together all my bank statements for the apparently lost years, and although I could not find evidence of having paid the sums quoted, I really did wonder, and still do, if it was not another almighty mistake like the last one. If only I had not thrown out all those old invoices when I moved house!

Meanwhile, a cheque written to France Telecom had been returned to them, unpaid, as it had been presented when the account was blocked. Again I knew nothing about this until Telecom informed me they were about to disconnect the line. No time to lose now, I had to cut my losses and pay up to have a fluid account and a working telephone. The conclusions to be drawn are, once again:

1. Do not jettison any local Commune invoices, particularly if you move away.
2. Check and double-check that services have your correct UK address.
3. Keep all bank statements – forever!

Although still dubious about the Bureau's claim, I am hoping that the purchaser of my town house will be sporting enough to share the taxes for that year. It is quite normal, but I have no expectations.

As three major French banks have branches in the UK, some may feel that it could well be easier to deal directly through them, by-passing the need to use the local branch nearest to your holiday home. I believe it to be the reverse. In the foreign section of most town banks, one or two managers operate, much as they do in the UK. Making personal contact with an individual is important and will prove to be invaluable. For example, officially a post-dated cheque cannot be presented as it must be paid in on the day you present it. However, a friendly personal manager will hold it until the correct date. If you present a sterling cheque, either payable to you, or drawn on your UK account, officially it will take about ten days to clear. This could mean difficulties if you are suddenly having to pay the plumber and your French account is threadbare. A friendly manager could credit you with francs immediately, thus saving you from a year's freeze-up.

Cheques

You cannot stop a cheque in France, as in the UK, by simply telephoning the bank. Much to my chagrin, I found this out the hard way, and as a consequence was obliged to go along with an undesirable purchase. When I mention this to French friends, they laugh. Buy something they don't really want? Never! So what do they do? They telephone the bank and report the loss of their chequebook. No problem. Easy, maybe, for a native, but with my banking history, I don't think I shall try that one – not yet.

Here are a few things you should know about the French cheque. If a cheque is more than six months old it is invalid, and what is more, you will probably never be told about it. If you make a mistake when writing a cheque, you cannot simply alter and initial it as you can in the UK. Whenever I have penned a signature to a crossed-out mistake, the recipient has always looked aghast, refused the cheque and asked for another. Should there be a discrepancy between words and figures on your cheque, the words prevail – because the French are a highly verbal people, do you suppose?

Obtaining a new chequebook can be a real pain. When a certain number of cheques have been used a new book, *carnet*, should be ordered, automatically, as in the UK. Alas, this does not always happen. New *carnets* in my bank and others are not sent on by post. You must collect personally. So do not wait until you have only a couple of cheques left in your book. The replacement may very well not have arrived, and you will immediately see the problems that could, and do, arise when there are bills to pay, and no cheques with which to pay them. My bank has left me stranded twice with no cheques and several bills. If you are a local, there is not much of a problem, but if the bills drop on to the UK mat there is. In this situation your personal manager can come to the rescue. Mine paid the EDF and France Telecom directly from my account, so reconnection charges were avoided. I now make a point of collecting, or more likely ordering, a new *carnet* when I call on my bank at the beginning of each holiday.

A few British friends with holiday homes have their French addresses printed on their chequebooks. They say it gives them more credibility when making local purchases. This may be so, but bank statements, and all other communications, will in this case undoubtedly be sent to the French address. Personally, I have had no problems with my British address on French cheques, although I have noticed over the past year or two that identification is being asked for more frequently, especially in the supermarkets. Cashiers are always surprised to learn that we do not carry identity cards. Yet while identification may be asked for, the rules about what form is acceptable are hardly rigid: on one occasion I was reduced to using my Equity Card, and it was accepted without question.

Don't ever be persuaded to open a *coffre* – a safe deposit box – at the bank. Some years ago, I sold a house and was due to receive that usual small percentage of cash from purchaser to vendor. For those who don't know, the money changes hands with the oblique connivance of the *notaire*, who goes to the loo at that point. He returns to the office, whistling nonchalantly, avoiding two pairs of shifty eyes, and the house sale and purchase procedure is finalised, with ne'er a mention of what went on when the *maître* was suddenly taken short. Unfortunately, I was unable to be present at this event which, I do assure you, though not strictly legal, sits very comfortably and amicably on the spongy parameters of the law. The estate agent volunteered to stand proxy – naturally, she didn't want to miss a sale. She insisted I open a *coffre* at the bank where the money could be deposited, and not by herself, too unethical, but by a friend whom I should designate. This I did, and gave the friend the key to my *coffre*.

After all the legalities were complete, the friend turned up at the bank with the money and the key. Alas, my banker, who had been apprised of the plan, had a headache that day, and his understudy sent the friend packing. It was not her *coffre* was it? She sensibly put the cash into her bank account and wrote me a cheque. So far so good.

A few months later, she moved house, and left word that the key to the *coffre* had been lost in the move. *Tant pis!* I was not using the *coffre* anyway. It was not until four years had elapsed that I realised I was paying £30 a year for the privilege of having this impregnable hole in the wall. I asked the bank for a duplicate key. They did not possess one. Not even head office had one. I was about to abandon all hope and write to the President when my banker suggested calling in an explosives expert. This I thought was rather drastic, but he assured me that the explosion would be confined to my *coffre*, and would not detonate the entire bank. I did not know an explosives expert, at least no one who openly professed such talent, but my manager did. Thus a freelance exploder from the Montpellier region was contacted. It would cost me £60, but so much better, said my manager, than paying out £30 each year. He was right of course, and so the date was fixed. On Wednesday morning at 11.00 a.m., I was to be at the bank to meet the exploder. The director of the bank, the securities clerk and my personal manager were waiting in the foyer. It was like the royal command. We stood in line, silently, the director checking his watch. At precisely 11.01 a.m, a small, dapper man dressed in black, carrying a large attaché case, marched up the steps into the foyer, where the reception committee was waiting. He was known to the director, introduced to the others, and last of all, to me.

He smiled. 'Ah yes, Madame. You are the owner of the locked *coffre* – yes? And you have lost the key?'

Feeling like an admonished schoolgirl, I nodded, blushing. Then he nodded to the director, who nodded to the securities clerk. They began to walk away, I started to follow.

'No, not yet,' said my manager. 'They will call you when they are ready.' I watched, fascinated. The director unlocked a heavy door at the far end of the *vestibule*. The three men disappeared down a flight of stairs. A few minutes later, the director and the securities clerk reappeared.

The director smiled. 'Please go down, Madame. Monsieur

is waiting for you.' My imagination was running riot, but naturally I obeyed, and walked down the thickly-carpeted stairs to a softly-lit cream and beige room. Had it not been for the walls, veneered from floor to ceiling with small *coffres*, the room could have been a *salon* rather than a vault. The director stood at the top of the stairs. 'I shall leave you now, with Monsieur,' he said, disappearing out of the door and locking us in. Monsieur had taken his jacket off, and was examining a *coffre*, which I presumed was mine, although I had never set eyes on it before this moment. On the floor lay his open attaché case. It was crammed with all sorts of gadgetry: presumably everything a professional exploder required.

He was very chatty, and obviously an expert because he recounted how he had twice been summoned to a London city bank to do some exploding, and on another occasion to a large insurance company. I didn't dare ask, but hoped his summoning had come from the management on each occasion. He then became very serious, and explained how much explosive he would need to use. Too much, and we could both be blown up. He laughed. I didn't.

'Stand back,' he said, after a few moments of fiddling and executing some deft surgery on the lock. I needed no telling. I was already cowering in a corner. There was a small 'pouff' and the *coffre* sprang open. It was empty, of course. He asked me to examine the damage, and was justly pleased that it was minimal. Then, on the intercom, he called the director, who unlocked the door and let us out. By now several customers had gathered in the area round the vault door. Maybe they saw us go in, or maybe they heard the 'pouff'. It was certainly more interesting than queuing.

In the foyer, the exploder politely shook hands, and assured me that should I ever again require his services, he would be happy to oblige. He had to hurry now, as he was off to another explosion that afternoon. The box had cost me a total of £200. So much for *coffres* and keys!

Bank Charges, Interest and Transferring Funds

Bank charges in France vary from bank to bank, and from region to region, but across the board there is little to choose between them. For example, Credit Agricole in the south-east charge you nothing to open an account, but will list their other charges according to the work involved.

If you can afford to have money sitting in a French bank, why not let it work for you? There is an ordinary savings account, *epargne*, which gives instant access at 4.5 per cent interest.

Another account well worth considering is SICAV, which, in March 1993, was offering an 8 per cent return on the investment. To open this account you will need 250F. There are no rules, and you may draw out your investment money as and how you wish. For this account, the bank will deduct 112F per annum.

For many years I have been exploring the various means of transferring money from the UK to France. English banks will transfer your money into francs by debiting your sterling account and sending the value in francs to your French account. Up to a sum of £5000, Barclays, for example, charge £11 for this service. Credit Agricole in London will take your sterling cheque or cash, up to the value of £5000, convert it into francs, and despatch them to your French account. They charge £8.50 for this service. Over £5000, they charge £3 per £1000.

Credit Agricole in London does not operate as a High Street trading bank, holding private accounts, but rather as a commercial bank, changing sterling cheques into francs at the commercial rate and transferring the sum to your French bank. As from May 1993, Credit Agricole accept sterling cheques for exchange and transfer only on a standing order basis, charging £6 per transfer, or less should you be happy with a quarterly standing order. The Co-operative Bank, on the other hand, has very competitive transfer charges. At the time of writing they are better than any other UK bank. They accept sterling for transfer at any time and exchange at the commercial rate. However to have a standing order arrangement you will be expected to open an account with them.

The quickest way of replenishing your French account is by telegraphic transfer, from your UK account, but this is expensive. See the table below for Credit Agricole's time-scale for types of cheque or cash conversion and transfer. These time-scales apply solely to Credit Agricole in the UK. If you shop around to find the best value for the shortest time, the following table will at least serve as a point of reference.

Type of Payment	No of days to Clear	No of days for funds to arrive in France
Personal or company cheque	6 working days	+1 to 2 working days
Cheque issued by building society or banker's draft below £20000	1 working day	+1 to 2 working days
Cheque issued by building society or banker's draft above £20000	3 working days	+1 to 2 working days.

Air mail transfers from your own bank take about ten days, and charges are particular to each bank.

Another method of payment is with a French franc draft. If you have a bill to pay, either for a service or to an individual, Credit Agricole will transfer the francs directly into the payee's account. You have to go to the bank in person, with either a banker's draft, a building society cheque or cash (up to a maximum of £5000), plus personal identification. The charge is £12.50 for sums below £5000, and £15 for sums above £5000. This method takes four working days to clear.

Transferring funds in francs is the cheapest way, sending sterling cheques is not. Here are copies of two French bank slips detailing transfer charges. Both are dated 1992, but each has a slightly difference *cours* (rate of exchange).

Transfer of sterling cheque

Montant GBP	150,00
Cours	9, 79450000
Contrevaleur	1469,18
Frais du Correspondant	0,00
Com. Change	65,00
TVA 18,600%	12,09
Com. Negocia	60,00
TVA 18,600%	11,16
Net Franc	1320,93

Even with a relatively high rate of exchange a sterling cheque of £150 loses about 10 per cent when exchanged in this way.

Transfer of francs from UK bank

Montant FRF	19575,00
Frais du Correspondant	0,00
Net Devise	19575,00
Cours	1,00000000
Contrevaleur	19575,00
Com. Change	0,00
TVA 18,600%	0,00
Com. Paiement	60,00
TVA 18,600%	11,16
Frais	0,00
TVA 18,600%	0,00
Net Franc	19503,84

As you will see, the percentage lost on this exchange, even allowing for the sterling paid out for the facility in the UK, is little more than 2 per cent.

Some regional banks in France charge upon receipt of funds from abroad, even if the funds are in francs. Although banks may have the same name, like Credit Agricole, or Credit Lyonnais, it is worth noting that they are not homogenous enterprises.

In the UK we expect Barclays, Lloyds and NatWest, for example, to have the same rates of interest and scale of charges in Torquay, Cardiff or Manchester. Not so in France. All regional banks, though sharing a name, are autonomous, each with its own rules and scale of charges.

For example, the Paris Isle de France Credit Agricole has abandoned all charges on francs transferred from abroad, so Paris could be cheaper than rural France. It is a sound idea to find out what your local bank's charges are before you commit yourself, and possibly your mortgage, to it.

Cash Cards and Credit Cards

If your fiscal standing *vis à vis* your French bank is good and steady, you will doubtless be offered a cash card immediately. In my case it took a few years. Of course, the card has proved invaluable, primarily because there are so many bank holidays in France that not only coincide with family holidays, but also with the builder's bill.

Recently my bank installed a super-sophisticated machine. As I suffer from numerical dyslexia, when the computerised display insisted that I return to square one, again and again, I naturally thought that either I had made a mistake in punching in the pin number or the account was in trouble. Eventually a kind cashier, like a boy scout taking an old lady across the road, explained the problem. It appears that these super machines are *de rigueur* now, so remember, after you have given the monster your details, and you still appear to be in favour, press the '*verifier*' button. Only then will your request be processed. Simple really, but confusing at the time.

A few months ago, I was concentrating so much on the new process that I punched in the wrong pin number. Of course, the machine swallowed my card. In my bank there is a particular cashier who gives advice, solace and comfort to those whose cards have been eaten. He was most apologetic that the key to this microchip monster was not in his possession. However, every Tuesday and Friday, an official with a key – from Montpellier again – arrived to open it up and retrieve lost cards. I wondered whether it was the exploder branching into modern technology. I was asked to come back on Wednesday, which I did, but once more the cashier was apologetic. The car carrying the key man from Montpellier had broken down, so the machine remained locked. But next week? I was returning to the UK the following day, so I had to wait until the next holiday to claim my card. Never mind, what use are French francs in Battersea?

With a good fiscal record, your bank could reward you with a Carte Bleu or Carte Verte, French credit cards. Personally, I have enough trouble with my Barclaycard without extending my credit frontiers to the continent. And the bad news is that in France you have to clear your debts every month, and we all know how seriously they view banking. Perhaps the Banque de France is more lenient with offending natives, but a foreigner? I am not convinced that Monsieur Guillotine's descendants haven't another trick up their sleeves.

Chapter Nine

Building Your House

For those already committed to a French holiday home, and for those merely thinking about it, location is always a serious consideration. While short journeys from the coast are very agreeable when the family is young, never lose sight of the fact that children grow up – fast – and that in a few years you will probably be using your home more *à deux* than *en famille*. As a general pattern, in later years the *famille* choose to visit when you are not there. Then the running battle about who bagged which dates first begins. You will unquestionably be *de trop*, you and your emulsion paint, and you may rest assured that paint and brush will be cast firmly aside during their sojourn.

If you are looking for a holiday home that could become a retirement home, choose the location you want. Children adapt, and will love it anyway.

Location

In the north-west, Brittany and Normandy, the climate is not too different from that of south-west England, mild and wet. But you will have the advantage of proximity to the UK, plus cheaper property, giving excellent value, interesting indigenous architecture and fabulous *cuisine*. House prices will probably increase when the Channel Tunnel becomes a living organism. In this region there are excellent beaches, spas, including a wonderful thalassotherapy centre at Pornichet; interesting towns like Nantes, Angers and Rennes, as well as the coastal resorts.

Moving south of Paris to Orléans and the Loire, the climate is certainly milder, and the riverscapes stunning, and there is scope for plenty of freshwater swimming. Architecturally, this is probably the most impressive region in the country, and two or three families can still buy a modest *château* between them with enough room to be quite separate and never meet unless they wish to.

The area around Fontainbleau, which boasts kilometres of forest, is full of interest and history. Commuter proximity to Paris may be an added advantage. However, there is a period of horrendous traffic congestion, from Sunday afternoon until midnight, to be avoided. This is when the whole of Paris returns from a DIY weekend at the *maison secondaire.*

East of Calais, as far as the Swiss border, and southwards as far as Lyons, is a region less populated by Brits and holiday homes. For my money it almost rivals the south (except for sunshine hours). Slightly dryer than its western counterpart, the area between Reims and Dijon is particularly beautiful, the Ardennes forming a stunning backdrop. Langres, de Gaulle's home, is a delightful town, set in the midst of four large lakes. If it's solitude and fishing you want, plus an easy drive from the coast, visit Langres first. Property in this region in 1989 was very reasonable, and as the French have had a property *crise* similar to ours, I would be surprised if prices have changed at all. In Langres, for example, a five-bed, shuttered, detached house with garage and garden was 300,000F. Just south of Langres, near St Dizier, the idyllic Lac du Der Chantecoq, with a shingle beach, swimming, sailing and fishing, is enveloped in absolute tranquillity. Villages a short distance away are well-kept, and worth looking at. One is so archetypal that it almost resembles a film set.

Driving through this area a few years ago, before the recession, I saw a glorious *château*, with extensive grounds, for sale. At the time I was living in a sought-after area of London, and I knew that if I sold up, I could buy the *château* and have some change. The temptation was enormous. I often wonder about what might have been, but I suppose being a *châtelaine* in a non-centrally heated pile in mid-winter is not quite so romantic.

Cambrai, to the west, is another of those attractive market towns near the coast. Here I saw a small *manoir* with six beds and a swimming pool for 780,000F. Going south again from here, you reach Burgundy, six or seven hours from the coast, and the weather becomes warmer.

Across to the west from this point is the area most beloved of the British: Bergerac and the Dordogne, the first British colony of post-revolution France. It is very green, warm and beautiful, but perhaps a little too wet for those who prefer a dry clime. Though lovely in summer, the winters can be very wet and foggy. The Atlantic coastline from La Rochelle to Bordeaux is spectacular, but the ocean is colder than the Med. There are relatively cheap properties to be found in the dozens of coastal villages around here. Friends have recently bought a delightful, solid, *en bon état* seaside village house for £21,000. The vendors even left most of the furniture.

Towards the centre of the country is the Massif Central. My

own feeling is that it is lovely to look at and explore, but perhaps not the best place for a holiday home. In winter many roads are impassable with heavy snowfalls for weeks at a time. Even in May, there is snow on the high ground. Many small towns and villages on the lower levels carry snow warnings.

While Clermont-Ferrand is another unlikely location for a holiday home, the Auvergne, particularly the Haute Savoie, is eminently suitable. Property is still cheap, although you will probably have to spend on extensive renovation. Summers here are usually hot and dry, and in winter there is skiing, cross-country, *de fond* and downhill. The ski centres are not busy, and ski and drag lifts are very cheap.

Further south, towards the Pyrenées, there are large towns like Toulouse (with airport) and Cahors. The weather is warmer and drier the nearer to the coast and to Spain you travel. It is a varied region with vineyards in the centre and south, an attractive coastline, and Biarritz to the west.

Carcassonne is another city of great historical interest and unique architecture. There are several ski centres nearby, and transport by road, air and rail is excellent. A holiday home here, in the south-west, is extremely well-placed, with skiing in winter, swimming in summer, and Spain on the doorstep.

It even offers interest to rugby fans: few aficionados of rugby will not have heard of Béziers, the home of French rugby. There are some great *équipes* in the south. In Béziers there is a statue to the man who brought rugby to the French, and taught them how to play it – a Welshman, from my home town. They have much to thank us for!

Moving east towards the Rhône valley, you have a perfect combination of climate and interest. Montpellier, with the oldest

Oxbridge by the Med. Here are stunning, recently-constructed blocks of domestic architecture, built in the classical tradition – a combination of Nash and Palladian.

The Roman legacy is very pronounced: Nîmes, Orange and the Pont du Gard are fine examples. The coastline includes the Carmague, where old shambly fishing ports rub shoulders with the ultra-modern Port Carmague and the pyramid-shaped condominiums of La Grand Motte. A little to the north are the spectacular gorges, grottos and the Cirque de Navacelles. Alès is the gateway to the vast nature reserve of the Cevennes, the cradle of the French Resistance in the Second World War. A holiday home in this region gives you access to the Carmargue and the coast, as well as to winter skiing on Mont Aigoual.

House prices are a little higher than in the west, especially around Avignon, but much lower than the Riviera. This is wine-lovers' country: Côtes du Rhône, Tavel, Châteauneuf du Pape. The climate is dry and hot in summer with the mistral blowing in certain seasons. Winter is short, but can be very sharp. Recently there has been snow, for the first time in living memory in some places.

East of Marseilles, the clip joints of the Côte d'Azur loom large. These southern coasts, for so long the stamping ground of English aristos, still maintain inflated prices to match the clientele. Glorious scenery and climate, where for the price of a house anywhere else you can buy a mobile home.

But in the Var, the Riviera's hinterland, there is reasonably-priced property to be found, and your money will buy more. There are quite lovely villages in this region, and you are only a few hours away from Italy.

If you are still just thinking about buying a *maison secondaire*, and before you lose your heart to that idyllic little stone house in the woods – only £12,000 – consider:

1. Being there alone in winter.
2. Adolescent offspring.
3. Proximity to food shops.
4. Proximity to neighbours – very important for absent householders.

I know of many parents, myself included, who have been faced with the choice between moving to the nearest town or village or spending the entire summer holiday playing chauffeur to teenagers who suddenly knew every minor within a radius of ten kilometres and upon whom the social sun never seemed to set. After two seasons of sitting almost nightly at a pavement café in the nearby town, waiting for my discoing daughters, I decided to sell up and move to civilisation. It had become embarrassing: I must have looked like a woman of the night, always touting for passing trade (and not getting any).

If you would like to spend Christmas Day in shirtsleeves, choose somewhere south of Lyons. If you cannot cope with the frequent intense heat of a Mediterranean summer go for the mid-west or central regions, avoiding the mountains, unless you love them. I have many British friends, now retired, who spend May, June and part of July and September to October in their southern holiday homes, avoiding the hottest months. A climatic halfway mark between Brittany and Provence would probably be the north-east, south of Reims. The choices are endless. France is a big country.

When you have made friends in an area, it is not such a good idea to move out of it, not for us bi-annuals and immigrants, anyway. I have moved house three times, but always within the same area, so I have kept friends and only changed neighbours.

Building Your Own House

Land prices in France are as varied as the length of a piece of string, depending on their location, but if you have found your favourite patch the next step is to make sure it is *terrain constructible* (building land). To find out you must visit the Mairie. Since planning departments have been decentralised, permission for development and change rests largely with the local mayor, and the Equipement.

If the land is *constructible*, you are given a *certificat d'urbanisme*, which states that the surface of the land has been authorised for building. The next step is to obtain a *permis de construire*. Unless your French is fluent and you are completely *au fait* with architectural and surveying terminology, you will need help to fill in these forms. For this planning application you will need a drawing of the projected building with details of the roof tiles, colour and shape, and the colour of the exterior rendering. Provided your house will not be an eyesore, and will blend into the general tone of the area, your planning permission will take about two months to come through. Don't forget that all municipal and local government offices either shut down completely in August or operate with a skeleton staff.

Once you have planning permission, it is valid for two years. When the building is complete ask for a *certificat de conformité*, which simply confirms that you have built to the original agenda set out in the planning application. After a period of three years, if the authorities suddenly discover a feature of the house that was not on the original plan, legally they can do nothing about it.

If you decide to sell up in less than five years, TVA (VAT) is payable. The trouble with building your own house is finding the time to pop over and supervise. I know several people who have been very unlucky in their choice of builder, and have consequently come severely unstuck. If this house is to be your retirement home, you will have an urgent need to keep a watchful eye on the construction. The best plan by far is to use a local architect, preferably one who speaks some English. Although this has been calculated to add 12 to 15 per cent to the total bill, it is well worth it in reducing the stress factor alone.

Make it very clear to your architect and his workforce how you intend to pay, whether upon completion of the work, or in instalments as predesignated sections of the building are completed. Always make sure you have fully inspected a completed section of the work before you pay up. Remember, the *certificat de conformité* will be in your name, and the buck stops with you. Your choice of architect will be fundamental to the project's success. Much will rest upon his shoulders, so a well-recommended professional is worth searching out.

Renovating Old Properties

Planning permission for renovation of an old property is only required if changes are to be made in the external shape of the building. When I applied to the Mairie for permission to take off the front part of my roof in order to make a roof terrace, I was given pages of application forms. The mayor and his aide helped me fill them in, and to save time I delivered them personally to the city department which deals with planning. At the mayor's request I had taken several photographs of the façade of the house, and then made a drawing of what it would look like with a roof terrace perched on top. Apart from the top of a sun brolly, there was little or no difference to the aspect of the house. The regulation height of the walls effectively conceals the terrace and anything on it. As well as the drawing, I also supplied, again at the mayor's request, a scale plan of the house, ground and first floors, plus the projected terrace. The city office could see the plans had not been drawn by a professional.

In the event, because the renovation would make no effective difference to the house exterior, he signed the plans, kept a copy for the files, and referred me back to the mayor, as it was he, the mayor, who would give the final permission.

In some cases, as in the UK, the areas of division are a little woolly, so the mayor was playing safe by sending me to the city department (see Chapter Two). If you have a listed house, nothing can be done to the exterior or interior without permission.

Apartments

There is no leasehold in France and as a flat-dweller you will be a *co-propriétaire*. Before you buy, you will have a copy of the house rules – *règlement de co-propriété* – which spell out your obligations and liabilities. You will also be given a list of charges. The block is usually divided into *lots* and each *lot* has its share of responsibility in the communal areas. In the rules concerning payment you will be told:

1. The service charges based on your *lot*, and when they should be paid.
2. What you may or may not do.
3. Rules about management meetings.

4. Meetings of flat-owners.

5. What happens if the block is damaged by fire or storm.

In fact, the organisation is very similar to blocks of flats in the UK where tenants share the freehold.

There is always an AGM, but usually British flat-owners are absent. If you have something to say, or a point to make, you are allowed to appoint a proxy.

In some condominiums the owner must conform to a certain type of window blind, and is prevented from painting the exterior of the flat, including the balcony, which is regarded in the rules as a communal area. You may keep domestic pets, let the flat, or use it for professional purposes.

Service charges are payable quarterly, and it is a very serious matter if you fall in arrears. For all flat-owners it is far better to have separate services. Many older flats have communal hot water and central heating, which is a little unfair on holidaymakers, who will pay just as much as residents toasting their toes in mid-winter. One last point: all flat-owners' meetings are in French, and all reports will be sent to you in French. And of course you should know what is going on and what decisions have been taken in your name. It takes great determination to plough through an AGM report in English. So keep a dictionary to hand, and a free week!

Chapter Ten

Community Life

Medical Care

As everyone who travels abroad knows, British nationals may have to pay for medical care received in the EEC, but if so they are reimbursed on their return to the UK because of reciprocal international arrangements. In France, just make sure that your doctor is fully French NHS – some are half private and half state. If you remember to take out medical insurance, all treatment will be free of charge and you will avoid having to fill in all those forms when you return. So much for the mechanics – what about the quality?

Several years ago very good friends, a surgeon and his wife, a doctor, decided, as they were getting older and spending more time in France, to look into French medicine – surgery, hospitals, and general medical care – with both a professional view and a personal eye on the future. They came up with a glowing report. Naturally, as they are Scots, Edinburgh has the best hospital in the UK, if not the world, but when they put Montpellier on a par with that of Albion's fair city, it had to be good. As a matter of fact, Montpellier attracts some of the best medical skills in the world, as it is a well-endowed centre for advanced research. Whenever there is anything new in the treatment of cancer, Montpellier will have it. Local French hospitals are very good, and nursing care is excellent. Another good friend, a former nursing sister, retired with her husband to France. He became terminally ill, and she cannot speak too highly of the care given to both patient and family during those trying weeks by a local hospital.

Montpellier hospital is very large and houses a flourishing medical faculty, continuing the tradition begun in the Middle Ages. Whenever we have required medical treatment in France the response has been instant and efficient. Resident British friends say there is never more than a three-week wait to see an NHS surgeon. Emergencies are dealt with instantly – hard to believe when you are used to the UK. Operations, even those classified as non-urgent, have no long waiting-lists.

A resident British friend's old mum flew out for a holiday. Purely by chance – the plane was delayed – she took out medical insurance at the airport. Within a few days of being in France she fell and bruised her bad hip – she had been on a hip replacement waiting-list in the UK for two years. She told the French doctor, and he told her not to worry, they would do it. Within a week she was in hospital having her new hip. Afterwards she was taken off to a lovely convalescent home by the Med. Two weeks later she was driven to the airport, wheelchairs at the ready, and was put, with tender loving care, on to a plane for London. Although it cost nothing because of her insurance, the speed with which the operation was arranged, and the subsequent care she received were nothing short of admirable.

The French are great believers in the suppository. So never be alarmed when the doctor prescribes one for your headache, backache, bad knee... Never mind, suppositories don't irritate the stomach, and are absorbed faster ... at least, that's what they say.

Residency

As a citizen of the EEC, you have a right to live and work in member countries, although most countries, including France, like to keep tabs on their foreign workforce. If you wish to stay in France for periods not exceeding three months, you are free to do so without any formalities. Should you wish to take up permanent residence, you need not now apply for a *visa de longue durée*. However you will still require a *carte de séjour* for any visit of more than three months. These are obtainable from the Prefecture, the Mairie or the Commissariat de Police. Importing your furniture and effects pose no problem, but you will need an attestation of residence from the mayor of your Commune/town. Furthermore you must prove you are reasonably healthy with a medical certificate. The latter does seem to be somewhat flexible. Some friends were able to obtain a residency permit for their old nonagenarian aunt, who was going out to live with them. Immigration will also require you to sign a declaration at the bottom of an inventory of all goods, including your car, for which all documents proving ownership will be required.

If you are using a removal company, they will need to have photocopies of all documents including the first five pages of your passport, a contract of employment, if you are going to work in France, or a *carte de séjour*. The French Consulate have the answers to all questions and will send you all the relevant information and documentation – even on turning your British household pets into French residents. To assist us in our desire for employment/ retirement in the sun, they have issued a formal letter, which should be presented to your local Prefecture/Mairie/Commissariat, and which reads as follows:

Dear Sir/Madam,

As of the 1 July 1992 nationals of the member states of the EEC, who want to work, are retired or who will be inactive in France, no longer need apply for long stay or permanent residence visas before moving to France.

The resident permit (*carte de séjour*) is still required and you should apply for this directly to the Prefecture, Mairie or Commissariat de Police in the departement where you intend to reside, within three months of arrival in France.

I would strongly suggest that you contact the Prefecture before your move to France, to ascertain what documents will be necessary for an application for a *carte de séjour*.

Yours faithfully,

CONSULAT GENERAL DE FRANCE
A LONDRES

Not all Prefectures welcome immigrants with joyful open arms, particularly if the area is already heavily over-subsribed. I have heard of some who try to give immigrants subtle tests in French language, customs and literature, and of others who insist we foreigners take a course in French language at the local evening classes. And who can blame them, as they beaver daily under the eagle eye of Napoleon, omnipresent in bust, portrait or spirit in all French governmental buildings? In any case I personally feel it is mildly insulting for any British immigrant to arrive in France without having some idea of the language and the people who will be his/her neighbours. It's back to the old days of Empire, and everyone speaks English, don't they? However, to make sure the immigrant is understood when application is made for a *carte de séjour*, the French Consulate have translated their English letter into French. This can also be presented to the Prefecture/Mairie/Commissariat without fear of misunderstandings.

Making a permanent home in France makes you liable for French income tax, which is no doubt as rotten as ours. If you are receiving any money from pensions or investments, for example, you will need the services of a French accountant. There are some odder liabilities, particularly if the red tape gets in a tangle.

When our first house (the one with the *fosse*) had been plumbed and wired, we decided to buy a clapped-out dormobile, fill it with furniture and the children, and motor down. It was to be our first summer holiday in *chez nous*. The dormobile was nearer the end than we had thought, for we broke down on the motorway. We were obliged to spend two nights in what turned out to be an enchanting hotel on the river Sâone, which we have visited many times since. Eventually we left, towed by one of those flashing rescue trucks, and hours later rumbled into the hamlet. The old van was going to cost more than the purchase price to repair, as had the cost of the tow, which had cleared me of every franc I possessed. Thus we left the vehicle in the patch of barren land belonging, but not attached to, the house. It had to be the broken-down dormobile that was responsible, because two years later a couple of customs officers were seen inspecting it. By this time it was a stately home for a colony of mice, who had never had it so good. What exactly the customs men read into it is hard to tell, but a year later my husband received his call-up papers for the French army.

Perhaps they thought a deserter was living there with the mice – but my husband? His feet were too flat even for the Korean War, and would certainly have been hopeless kicking up sand with the Foreign Legion. Obviously, French intelligence knew nothing of the shape of his feet if he was summoned to do his National Service for France. He hadn't even done his National Service for Britain, but perhaps the British intelligence had actually donated him – ostensibly as a generous gesture, but in fact as a secret weapon to debilitate and disrupt the French army. Perhaps the old enemies were at it again, adopting a tactic to stir up trouble before anyone could utter European Community or Channel Tunnel, for this was 1974.

Anything was possible. In the event we decided to do nothing about it, even when the second summons arrived. After that we heard nothing. Clearly British intelligence had decided to let bygones be bygones and to hell with Burgundy. There was no other explanation. But it could happen to anyone – so be prepared.

Residency and Medical Care

If you are resident and working in France, you will be obliged to join the French NHS. What you pay depends on your income: there is a sliding scale of contributions.

The French NHS does not pay 100 per cent of medical bills, so to make up the shortfall, do as most of the French do and join an insurance scheme, a *mutuelle*. Your company will no doubt do it for you. If your French income is very high, you may be better advised to take out private medical insurance in the UK.

However, certain illnesses such as cancer, diabetes and heart problems do warrant a 100 per cent reimbursement.

Retirement, Residency and Medical Care

If you are retired and have your *carte de séjour* your UK pension will be sent to your French bank, or wherever you wish. Don't forget to inform your local DSS office in advance of your date of departure to allow you to register for health care immediately. As a pensioner, 80 per cent of your medical treatment will be free of charge, and the rest, *de rigueur*, through a *mutuelle*. Naturally, obtaining your 80 per cent involves form-filling. The DSS will give you form E121, which you must fill in and present to your local French Securité Social. Upon receipt you will be given a card and number. When a resident requires a doctor's visit, drugs from the chemist or treatment, X-rays, blood tests, etc., this is recorded, by the person giving the medical care, on a *feuille de soins*. Provided all treatment received has been verified and signed by the professionals involved, you will be reimbursed upon presentation of the *feuille de soins* at the cash desk of the local Securité Social.

Most of our British friends w've known since they bounced through their forties and fifties. Some of them are still bouncing, or at least ambling happily, through their sixties, seventies and more. In France they are now in their *troisième age*, a far more gracious nomenclature than 'OAP'. Each Commune provides dozens of activities for mind and body. There are walks, talks, discussions, lectures, digs, excursions. Many towns have university extension courses leading to diplomas. Lyons, for example, has a *faculté catholique* where the *troisième age* can enrol for courses. There is no open university scheme in France, but there are plenty of other opportunities for study and developing interests. There is a choice of holidays, too, not free, but at a reduced cost. Last year friends flew to Greece for a two-week holiday organised by the local *troisième age* group, and spas and health centres are other options. All activities and opportunities are open to British *troisième* agers. My nearest town is of special historical importance, so it is very common to see busloads of pensioners gathering in earnest groups to listen attentively to a short burst of history lecture from their guide. They always appear interested and happy to be learning something new, which seems to be not only a very positive approach to age, but life-enhancing. More than one can say of OAPs in smoke-filled bingo halls.

If you want more information a leaflet (SA29), *Your Social Security and Pension Rights in the EEC*, is available from the DSS Overseas Group, Newcastle-upon-Tyne NE98 1YX.

Alternative Medicine

The first time I was ill during a holiday my neighbour effected a cure. She gave me verbena leaves, which I brewed up into a *tisane*. On every market in France you will find a herb stall, and the keepers of such stalls are generally well-acquainted with herbal medical cures, and will listen to problems with the attention of a conventional practitioner. They have proved to be whizz-kids with all the insomniacs in the family, and those with perpetually gnawing stomach ulcers.

Herbal medicine in France is well-respected and accepted as part of an old, inherited tradition and folklore, and for years it has happily run alongside conventional medicine. Although we also have fringe herbal medics in the UK they are not nearly as commonplace as they are in France. It may be that France's rural heritage has had a stronger influence, and that folk medicine has been kept alive through oral tradition.

Homeopathy, too, has never had to fight for recognition as in the UK. It has long been an equal partner with conventional medicine. Even in small towns there will be a homeopathic chemist, who will also offer advice and remedies for ailments. I was once suffering from a bloodshot eye that looked like a sunset, the result of an allergy. The local homeopathic chemist sold me the most effective eye drops I have ever used.

The French Consulate confirms that every French hospital has a homeopathic department, and it is easy to find homeopathic doctors.

Your Will

The French have got it right in so many ways, not least when it comes to wills and beneficiaries. So many women in the UK have gone through a long marriage and painful divorce, only to find that his new 20-year-old bimbette wife inherits all, to the complete exclusion of the offspring of loins once wed. Not so in France. Parents and children have an absolute right to inherit most of your assets. The spouse is only included if the will says so. A French will would automatically leave 50 per cent to an only child, two thirds to two children, and three or more would have about three quarters. If the spouse is to live on in the house, and make free use of the assets, there is a clause which allows him or her to do so, but only for that spouse's lifetime. Thereafter the assets revert to the children.

If you are a resident Brit, domiciled in France, French inheritance law will apply, and you should make a French will. If you still have assets in the UK, you will need to make a UK will as well. However, because you are domiciled in France, your English assets will be dealt with by French law. But make it clear where you are domiciled, otherwise the Inland Revenue will come calling for booty as well.

If you are merely a holiday home-owner domiciled in the UK, your French house and bank account will still be subject to French law after you die. So make a French will. In order to protect your partner (for example, so that children of a former marriage don't suddenly appear and claim), you should always buy property jointly – *en tontine* – as in the UK. In France most couples buy as a common tenancy – *en division* – which after death follows the normal French inheritance legalities. If you buy *en tontine* the spouse may inherit the property and assets. In the case of divorce, once the UK solicitors have agreed which partner has the house, the other merely has to assign his or her half. The French *notaire* does the rest. This formality does not necessarily have to be linked with divorce.

If you buy *en division* you will avoid French inheritance tax, but it could lead to the family problems already discussed. If you buy *en tontine*, there will be no problems with lost or visible offspring, but there will probably be inheritance tax to pay.

Spouses and children pay no tax on the first 275000F. Physically or mentally handicapped beneficiaries pay no tax on the first 300000F.

If the death occurs in France, French tax rules allow six months for any estate tax to be paid. It may be paid out of UK assets, but if there are insufficient funds there, the authorities will arrange an instalment plan. If the death occurs outside France, the family has a year to pay it off.

As a single parent with two adult children, I was ushered into a local *notaire*'s office by anxious friends. I really need not have bothered. The *notaire* asked me if I intended to leave my home to cats.

'No,' I said, surprised.

He raised his eyebrows, and smiled. 'But all you English leave to cats and dogs, not your children.'

I assured him I was leaving only to my daughters. He told me there was no need for me to make a will. Everything would pass to them.

There are three types of French wills:

1. **Secret Will**. You may write this yourself, and sign it. Two witnesses should see you put it in an envelope and give it to the *notaire*. He signs the envelope and keeps it for your next of kin.

2. **Holograph Will**. Written in your own handwriting, signed and dated. No witnesses are necessary, as there should be no other writing on it but yours. It is better to give it to a *notaire* than to a bank, as your family may have difficulty in getting the bank to release it.

3. *Notaire*'s **Will**. The *notaire* dictates this to you. Your signature, plus the signatures of either two *notaires* or one *notaire* and two witnesses, are inscribed. Again, the *notaire* keeps the will.

Choosing a good *notaire* is vital to the expedition of family affairs. I frequently hear grumbles about the time French lawyers take to finalise wills.

You may write your will in English, and in the British manner with two witnesses, but it should be lodged in France because it deals with French assets and is subject to French law.

An executor in English law is someone who administers the estate. They do not exist in France, and there is no need for a British property owner to appoint an executor. The *notaire* is there to guide the next of kin through any problems arising.

The Social Scene

Brits who take the trouble to meet neighbours halfway are rarely disappointed. Alas, so many of our countrymen complain about so-called French reserve when they themselves barely nod to their neighbours and expect them to do the running. This attitude is high-handed and embarrassingly reminiscent of the days of the Empire.

Some Brits remain mum because of the language problem. But surely, if people choose to holiday on a fairly permanent basis in a particular country, it is their responsibility to learn a little of the language? Unfortunately, the antiquated notion that we are British and everyone else foreigners, even in their own country, still pervades to a degree. Only the other day, I heard strong complaints that hoteliers on the Normandy coast didn't speak English.

The complainers spoke not a word of French and had no intention of even trying. That type of bulldog arrogance is anathema to the French, and could well rekindle the Napoleonic Wars. I know whose side I'd be on.

Recently I have heard of some new, custom-built, all-British holiday villages in the Dordogne. Would it not be cheaper, and even more British, to have a chalet in Cornwall? Fortunately, the majority of holiday home-owners, and certainly the ones I know, are true Francophiles. They love the country, and the food, make valiant attempts with the language, and make good friends of local people. That doesn't mean that there is a constant exchange of cultures. Lunch and dinner parties and other social events can be very true Brit in the holiday season, partly because the residents want to see all the semi-residents, and the semis want to chat to the residents about builders and plumbers. The guests of both want to talk houses and prices, because they might want to join the club themselves next year.

Time was when a Brit need not have uttered a word of French during these lunch parties and *soirées*, because generally few French were invited, and those that were could speak English. However, as time has progressed so has everything else. Now there is always a good 50-50 mixture of French and British at these social functions. Perhaps it's to do with confidence and trust, the result of living alongside each other.

Neighbours

Anyone who has a holiday home in France knows the importance of a good relationship with the neighbours. French people are at first reserved, so don't be put off. They are genuinely interested in you, your family, and what you are doing to the house. Invite them in to see the changes and renovations. As they are all mad keen *bricoleurs* anyway, you could acquire some sound advice. Children make wonderful ambassadors, especially if there are French children for them to play with.

Ask your neighbours in for a pre-dinner drink. *Apéritifs* – pastis and cocktail biscuits from the supermarket – are all you will need. They will leave politely in time for you to eat. Once you know them it will be difficult to get anyone to leave before midnight.

Last time I was prepared, so I invited a good mixture, French and English, for 7.00 p.m. and made sure that we, like our French guests, had eaten well at lunch-time. As predicted we were clearing up at midnight.

In our first house, although the hamlet's indigenous population was very small, it grew in summer with visitors like ourselves. Parisians, we were told, but we had never seen them, until one evening. We were in the kitchen on the first floor, the windows open, and became aware of laughter and music somewhere in the distance. Suddenly the voices drew nearer, below the window in fact. Someone shouted: 'Hello English – please come to party.'

And that was the beginning of a really good friendship between four couples and their children. We stayed with them in Paris, they came to us in the UK. Almost every evening somebody would have some sort of social gathering. We were all, French and English alike, building our *maisons secondaires*. The villagers loved the summer when we all descended. The older ones would recount hair-raising stories of the Resistance, Nazi reprisals, Gestapo atrocities. Their friends and families had heard it all before, but we were new and eager to know about a living history that could never be found in books. Those summers gave us all a new lease of life.

From the outset we had the sense to leave the house keys with our neighbours, a delightful old couple who lived opposite. I recollect it was rather an act of courtesy and trust, than one of practical implications. In any case no one of sound mind would have wanted to venture near our dreadful *fosse*. So we set off back to the UK that first September morn, leaving shutters open, and possibly not secured. We were unused to shutters and at the time no doubt believed their purpose was mainly for effect, like the bidet. Within days of our departure the mistral arrived, causing utter havoc amongst man and beast. After a night and day of fierce clattering and banging, and keeping everyone awake, our good neighbours, plus the rest of the hamlet, decided enough was enough, *fosse* or no, they would have to get in and fix the shutters. Had they not done so, it is doubtful whether shutters and windows would have survived the onslaught. Always make sure 'shutters' features on the departure check-list.

When we moved into town, again we had good neighbours, but town life does not have the bonding, community feel of the village. During this period we found many delightful ex-pats who were a source of inspiration and help when everything seemed to spell trouble. There you'd be, up to your ears in debris, when a friendly voice would bid you down tools, bundle you into a car, and take you home to lunch. That is when good neighbours are most appreciated.

Always leave the house keys with someone, a neighbour, friend or builder, and ask them to look in from time to time. My present neighbours are wonderful. French and semi-retired, Eli is like a *concierge*, and makes regular inspections in my absence. He was particularly vigilant when the renovations were in full swing and would give me blow-by-blow reports. In summer there are always baskets of vegetables from their garden placed outside my door, and community life being the same wherever you go, there are short cuts to problems, bureaucratic and social, which only a local knows.

The trap that so many Brits, in the midst of modest renovations of their *maison secondaire*, fall into, is trying to keep up with the Joneses. There is this subtle, subliminal jockeying for best house, which attacks when they have left someone's stunning conversion and returned to their own half-done shambles. It can be depressing and disheartening. But be strong! Others will have more money to spend, enough to have everything to done for them, while you are up to the elbows in squalor. They may even have employed a real architect. So what? Don't be downhearted when those people from Kent show you their pool. Who wants a pool, anyway, with all that winter debris to clean out?

Don't be drawn into this property pecking order. Whenever a house is going through the birth pangs of restoration, at the outset of any social gathering on site guests are taken on a conducted tour. You will do it, we all do it, because this is constructive, and we learn from each other. You will hear 'oohs', and 'aahs', and 'Why don't we have one of those, darling?'

Always remember your budget. There's no hurry, so take your time. Some families spend years – ten, 15 – to restore their holiday homes. After all, it is a *maison secondaire*. If it becomes your permanent home, the situation will change. Most of the real stunners are permanent homes, anyway. As you have to have two and more of everything, how can you possibly have the silver plate and cut glass in France as well? Take heart. They are only furnishing one house.

Of course, there are Brits who manage to convert even *maison secondaires* into palaces, like my British friends in the village, who really are called Jones. They even have a pool, and the house is a beautifully-designed minimalism in cream and white. Whenever I return, after a visit, to my French Victorian maximalism with its strong colours, I feel dissatisfied, but not depressed. My house is period, theirs is a converted and extended stone house, with architect, of course. They are not DIYers, they can afford not to be, but their house gives inspiration. Next year I think I shall go minimalist too, in cream and white.

I make a point of inviting friends and neighbours to some sort of social gathering each holiday. At any given time, there could be a German couple retired to France – he fought at Leningrad – a retired British major, Second World War, a French woman whose father fought in the Resistance, a Belgian couple who remember the Nazi invasion plus a diverse assortment of young and old. This is surely what is important: the breaking down of natural hesitations, and national barriers, while preserving, and valuing, the differences.

And how important they are, those differences, for why else would we ever cross the Channel to La Belle France, and our *chez nous?*

Bonne Chance!

GLOSSARY

Here are a few words that may be worth knowing. If you already have a house in France, many of them will be known or at least ring bells. This is not intended to be anything more than a personal selection, so a good dictionary is a sound investment and, perhaps even better, a French manual on *bricolage* (DIY). This way, even if you are not a DIY boffin, you will be able to keep a professional eye on the workforce and its daily progress.

THE HOUSE

le domicile	home
la ruine	run-down property
le toit	roof
le toiture	roofing
la porte	door
les parois	partition walls
un grenier	attic, barn
le plafond	ceiling
la fenêtre	window
le sol	floor
la salle à manger	dining-room
la salle de bain	bathroom
le chambre à coucher	bedroom
la cusine	kitchen
la salle de séjour	living-room
le bureau	study
l'escalier	stairs
le main courant	banister
le palier	landing
le cloison contre l'humidité	damp course

FURNITURE

les meubles	furniture
l'armoire	wardrobe
les tiroirs	drawers
le table de toilette	dressing-table
le table de nuit	bedside table
le lit bateau	antique bed with cot sides and shaped ends
le lit de traverse	antique alcove bed, with one decorated cot side
la cuisinière	cooker
le frigo	fridge
le congelateur	freezer
le sac à poubelle	refuse bag
les volets	shutters

TOOLS

l'atelier	workshop
la scie	saw
le marteau	hammer
le ciseau à bois	wood chisel
le bédane	mortise chisel
le râpe	rasp
le rabot	plane
l'équerre droite	right angle
la fausse équerre	bevel square

173

le mètre pliant	folding rule	le tamis	riddle, sieve
le mètre-ruban	tape measure	la bêche	spade
le trusquin	mortise gauge	la pioche	pick
la clé à molette	adjustable spanner	la truelle de maçon	masonry trowel
		le ciseau de briqueteur	bricklayer's chisel
la pince universelle	pliers	le ciseau de maçon	masonry chisel
la tenaille	pair of pincers	le marteau d'emballeur	claw-hammer
le couteau universel	cutter (Stanley knife)		
		WOODWORK	
le réglet métallique	metal rule	le contre-plaqué	plywood
le jeu de clés	set of spanners	les assemeblages	joints
le coupe-verre	glass-cutter	- enfouchement	dovetailing
la paire de ciseaux	pair of scissors	- tenon et mortaise	tenon and mortise
le tournevis	screwdriver	- rainure et languette	tongue and groove
la vis	screw		
le clou	nail	le bois massif	solid wood
le maillet en bois	wooden mallet	le chêne	oak
la vrille	gimlet	le pin	pine
le vilebrequin	bit-brace	le hêtre	beech
la mèche	bit, drill	le vernis	varnish
- à bois	wood drills	la quincaillerie	hardware
- à béton	concrete drill	la charniére	hinge
la perceuse électrique	electric drill	le loqueteau	small latch, catch
le foret pour le metal	metal drill		
la brosse métallique	wire brush	ELECTRICITY	
la lime	metal file	Le courant électrique	electric current
le fer à souder	soldering iron	Courant alternatif et continu	AC/DC
l'étau d'établi	fixed vice	la phase	live
la lampe a souder à gaz	blow lamp	le neutre	neutral
la brosse	brush	la terre	earth
la brosse d'encollage	pasting brush	les unités de mesure	units of measure
la brosse à maroufler	wallpaper brush	le volt	volt
la roulette à joint	roller for wallpaper joints	l'ampère	amp
		le watt	watt
le rouleau à peinture	paint roller	le court-circuit	short circuit
le gratttoir triangular	triangular scraper	le disjoncteur	circuit-breaker, cut-out switch
le niveau à bulle	spirit level		
le fil à plomb	plumb-line	le conjoncteur	mains switch
la ficelle	string	le coupe-circuit à fusible	fuse
l'éponge	sponge	le coupe-circuit principal	main fuse
la burette	oil-can	l'éclairage	lighting
la forte agrafeuse	staple-gun	l'alimentation électrique	electrical supply
la scie circulaire	circular saw	le tension du courant	voltage
la ponceuse	sander	la baguette	cable cover
la pelle	shovel	le socle	insulating base

la fiche	plug	**PLUMBING**	
le télérupteur	light switch	les tubes de cuivres	copper piping
le douille	light socket	les tuyaux en PVC	PVC pipework
une fusible à cartouche	cartridge fuse	les raccords	joints
faire sauter les plombs	blow the fuses	le siphon	trap (of a drain)
un fil fusible	fuse wire	les colliers	fixing clips
une porte fusible	fuse-box	le robinet	tap
la prise	socket/power point	un mélangeur	mixer-tap
		le raccord coudé	bend joint
la prise de terre	earth socket	le manchon	sleeve
		la vidange	draining

MASONRY

Le mur	wall	les elements sanitaires	sanitary ware
le muret	low wall	une baignoire	bathtub
l'enduit	plaster coating	une douche	shower
le plâtre	plaster	un cuvette de w.c.	toilet pan
le plâtroir	plastering trowel	un lavabo	wash basin
un bouclier	plastering hawk	la fosse septique	septic tank
la chaux	lime	tout à l'égout	on main drainage
le ciment	cement	l'étanchéité (à l'eau)	waterproofing
les agrégats	aggregates	l'evacuation	waste-water drainage
le sable	sand		
les gravillons	loose chippings, fine gravel	le débouchage des canalisations	unblocking the drains
les cailloux	pebbles	un fuite	leak
les pierres concassés	crushed stones	un coulage	substantial leak
les moellons	quarry stones	l'évier	sink
le seau	bucket		
le béton	concrete	**WALL DECORATION**	
la marche	step	le papier peint	wallpaper
la dalle	paving stone	les dalles de mirroir	mirror tiles
le pavage	pavement, paved area	la table à encoller	pasting-table
		la colle	paste
le mortier	mortar	l'escabeau	step-ladder
le brique	brick	une decolleuse	paper stripper
la brique creuse	hollow brick	un papier préencollé	ready-pasted wallpaper
la brique réfractaire	fire-proof brick		
le foyer	fireplace	le tissu	fabric covering
le parpaing	breeze-block	le velour	velvet
le terrassement	digging	la toile de jute	hessian
une tranchée	trench, ditch	la soie	silk
la bétonnière	concrete mixer	le molleton	flannel, felt
le béton armé	reinforced concrete	le carrelage	tiling
		le carreau de faïence	ceramic tile
le linteau	lintel	une carelette/ un coupe-carreau	tile-cutter

175

le liège	cork	le conduit	ventilation shaft
la peinture	painting	un boisseau	chimney-flue tile
le térébenthine	turpentine	le poêle	stove
un aspect mat	matt finish	le poêle-cheminée	modern
un aspect velouté	silk finish		Scandinavian-
un aspect satiné	eggshell finish		type wood-
			burning stove

FLOOR COVERINGS

la moquette	carpet	le convecteur	convector heater
le tapis	rug	l'accumulateur	storage heater
une moquette avec une	foam back carpet	le chauffage central	central heating
sous-couche en mousse		la chaudière	boiler
synthétique		le chauffage à air pulsé	hot-air heating
		le chauffeau	water heating
		la chaudière à gaz	gas-fired boiler

INSULATION

l'isolation	insulation	la chaudière au mazout	oil-fired boiler
l'isolant	insulating	la chaudière au charbon	charcoal-burning
	material		boiler
les planchers bas	floor boards	la chaudière	multi-fuel boiler
les murs extérieurs	external walls	polycombustible	
les combles	loft area	l'energie solaire	solar energy
les rampants	roof arches	le reglage de la	temperature
le lambris	panelling,	témpératature	control
	wainscoting	le robinet thermostatique	thermostatic
la laine de verre	fibre-glass		radiator tap
les chevrons	rafters	le programmateur centralisé	centralised
le plaque à plâtre	plaster board		programmer
le liège en particules	cork particles	le robinet de purge	air release tap
la vermiculite	mica particles		
un cloison	dividing wall	## HOUSE PROTECTION	
le calfeutrage	draught-proofing	la clôture	fencing
le double-vitrage	double-glazing	le grillage	wire-netting
les joints an mousse	foam strips	le parterre	flower-bed
le bourrelet en caoutchouc	rubber beading	la pelouse/gazon	lawn
la plinthe	skirting	l'haie	hedge
le joint d'étanchéité	draught-excluder	le poteau	post
la charnière	hinge	le portail	gateway
le chambranle	door-frame	le portillon	gate
		le mur de clôture	boundary wall
		un muret en pierre sèches	dry-stone wall
## HEATING		la fermeture	home security
le chauffrage	heating	l'entrebailleur à chaine	security chain
la cheminée	fireplace	le verrou	bolt
le foyer (l'âtre)	hearth	le serrure	lock
le contre-coeur	fire-back	la gâche	catch of a lock, or
le cendrier	cinder tray		striking plate